WOMEN IN SCHOOL LEADERSHIP

HOW TO ORDER THIS BOOK

BY PHONE: 800-233-9936 or 717-291-5609, 8AM–5PM Eastern Time

BY FAX: 717-295-4538

BY MAIL: Order Department
Technomic Publishing Company, Inc.
851 New Holland Avenue, Box 3535
Lancaster, PA 17604, U.S.A.

BY CREDIT CARD: American Express, VISA, MasterCard

PERMISSION TO PHOTOCOPY–POLICY STATEMENT

Authorization to photocopy items for internal or personal use, or the internal or personal use of specific clients, is granted by Technomic Publishing Co., Inc. provided that the base fee of US $3.00 per copy, plus US $ .25 per page is paid directly to Copyright Clearance Center, 27 Congress St., Salem, MA 01970, USA. For those organizations that have been granted a photocopy license by CCC, a separate system of payment has been arranged. The fee code for users of the Transactional Reporting Service is 1-56676/93 $5.00 + $ .25.

WOMEN IN SCHOOL LEADERSHIP

Survival and Advancement Guidebook

ARETHA B. PIGFORD, Ph.D.
Associate Professor
University of South Carolina
Columbia, South Carolina

SANDRA TONNSEN, Ph.D.
Associate Professor
University of South Carolina
Columbia, South Carolina

TECHNOMIC PUBLISHING CO., INC.
LANCASTER · BASEL

Women in School Leadership
a **TECHNOMIC**® publication

Published in the Western Hemisphere by
Technomic Publishing Company, Inc.
851 New Holland Avenue, Box 3535
Lancaster, Pennsylvania 17604 U.S.A.

Distributed in the Rest of the World by
Technomic Publishing AG
Missionsstrasse 44
CH-4055 Basel, Switzerland

Copyright © 1993 by Technomic Publishing Company, Inc.
All rights reserved

No part of this publication may be reproduced, stored in a
retrieval system, or transmitted, in any form or by any means,
electronic, mechanical, photocopying, recording, or otherwise,
without the prior written permission of the publisher.

Printed in the United States of America
10 9 8 7 6 5 4 3 2 1

Main entry under title:
  Women in School Leadership: Survival and Advancement Guidebook

A Technomic Publishing Company book
Bibliography: p. 79
Includes index p. 85

Library of Congress Catalog Card No. 93-60093
ISBN No. 1-56676-017-8

*To the memory of
Gordon McAndrew
a true visionary, a constant source of inspiration, and a
staunch advocate for equity.*

Table of Contents

Foreword ix

Preface xi

Acknowledgement xv

Chapter 1: Women: Outsiders to the Good Ol' Boy Network 1

From Then to Now 1
Today's Administrator: A Profile 2
Defining a Woman's Place 4
Keeping Women in Their Place 5

Chapter 2: Barriers to the Good Ol' Boy Network 7

Internal Barriers 8
External Barriers 14
Effective Principals: More Feminine than Masculine? 16
Black Women Administrators: Their Experiences 16

Chapter 3: Breaking into the Good Ol' Boy Network 19

Know Yourself 20
Know the Job Market 25
Prepare Yourself 27
Implement Successful Job-Hunting Strategies 31

Conclusion   37

Chapter 4: Prospering in the Good Ol' Boy Network   38
Building and Maintaining Interpersonal Relations   39
Managing Time   41
Communicating   49
Dealing with Subordinates   55
Advice for Black Women   57
Conclusion   59

Chapter 5: Balancing Your Life   60
Keeping Current   61
Presenting a Professional Image   61
Managing Stress   63
Balancing Your Life: For Married Women   64
Balancing Your Life: For Single Women   72

Appendix   77

Bibliography   79

Index   85

About the Authors   87

Foreword

Women in School Leadership: Survival and Advancement Guidebook is a profoundly practical, but pragmatic book. The authors have ably drawn upon their experiences and the experiences of colleagues. The result is a handbook—a guide, if you will—for educational leaders. Indeed, aspiring as well as current female administrators will benefit immeasurably from a careful reading of this treatise.

The book defines the issues accurately in terms of barriers. However, it quickly follows with specific solutions. Seldom does a *how to* guide provide the degree of specificity contained in this work. This book is significantly enlivened by anecdotes and examples. The reader is exposed to a myriad of approaches for "making it" in the system. The Ol' Boy Network is masterfully exposed, then explored. The authors present clever strategies for managing time, assessing self, and balancing one's life. From outsiders to insiders, women are given healthy doses of tips and techniques.

At its base, this book is focused on leadership and ways of developing effective leadership skills and traits. An extraordinary ingredient is the place of personal development as it relates to the broader concept of leadership. This holistic view of viable leadership provides the reader with tools for evolving and developing. Regardless of one's "state of becoming," or whether one is experienced or inexperienced in administration, women will find here an able friend and a steady guide.

Such a document is long overdue. Women who heed the advice

will not only enter the hallowed halls of administration, they will flourish. When the Ol' Boy Network is inclusive rather than exclusive, education, our cherished profession, will be the richer. We owe it to our children to cultivate the best and brightest, notwithstanding gender, into leadership ranks. Women and men are indebted to Drs. Pigford and Tonnsen for their time, talent, and expertise in crafting both a journal and a guide.

I am honored to add my voice to the chorus who will applaud this noble effort.

Ruth B. Love, Ph.D.

Preface

Between the two of us, we have more than forty-two years of experience as professionals in education. During our careers, we've worked with our share of talented, bright women. Some have been teachers; others have been students in our classes; a few have been administrators. Indeed, far too few have expressed an interest in the challenge of school administration. And sadly, many—if not most—of those enrolled in educational administration programs have not seemed serious about seeking administrative positions. Many have taken our courses merely to renew their teaching certificates while others have been motivated by the salary increases awarded for earning a specified number of credit hours. We have learned in our personal conversations with some of these women that the few who are interested in becoming school administrators tend to prefer not to make their aspirations public.

As a result of our encounters, we recognized the need to provide women with a set of experiences that would be unique to them, and which would help to stimulate the confidence many of them seemed to lack. What resulted was the development of an institute called "Leadership Skills for Today's Female School Administrator," more commonly referred to as the "Women's Institute." Open to aspiring or newly appointed female school administrators, the institute provides women an opportunity to learn about the realities of school administration, to assess their leadership abilities and skills, and to develop a support network with women who are interested in, and who hold, positions of leadership. Institute participants work through simulations and role-playing activities requiring problem-solving and conflict-management skills. In addition, they are provided ongoing opportunities for interacting with each other as well as with successful women leaders. After only four years, we have come to appreciate the impact of the institute on the participants, as evidenced by comments such as:

- ''Not only has this course helped me improve my administrative skills, but it has helped me see my worth as a woman.''
- ''Every woman administrator needs this course!''
- ''This workshop gave me an opportunity to examine my strengths as well as my weaknesses. Unlike other professional workshops, the Women's Institute was geared to my development as an individual.''

Our involvement with the Women's Institute has reminded us of the issues, concerns, and fears many women face relative to school administration. In *Women in School Leadership: Survival and Advancement Guidebook,* we have coupled the information gained through the Women's Institute with our own personal experiences to provide practical suggestions, advice, and approaches for addressing problems faced by aspiring and practicing female school administrators.

While we make occasional references to research conducted by us and others, it was not our intent to write a scholarly piece. Instead, we have attempted to write a book that is readable and practical. To that end, we have provided lots of examples, samples, and anecdotes. In addition, we have included a discussion of an issue that has been virtually ignored—the unique experience of black women administrators. Due to the paucity of research on this topic, much of what we say about the experiences of black women administrators will be based on our own firsthand observations.

We speak to you from experience. Before becoming professors of educational administration, we held a number of positions in public education. Dr. Aretha Pigford, a black female, has served as a teacher in the public schools of New York City, a principal, and a university administrator. She has been married for twenty-four years and is the mother of a teenage son and daughter. Dr. Sandra Tonnsen, a white female, has served as a teacher and administrator at the high school, district, and university levels. She is divorced and has no children. Having experienced the realities of operating in a man's world, we will share many of our personal stories.

Throughout *Women in School Leadership: Survival and Advancement Guidebook*, we will use the pronouns "I" and "we." To relate an experience that we both shared, "we" will be used; to relate an experience that was unique to one of us, "I" will be used. We have tried to write each situation clearly so that, when needed, it is obvious which author's experience is being described. We hope you won't be confused.

Women in School Leadership: Survival and Advancement Guidebook is divided into five chapters. In Chapter 1 we provide a brief historical perspective of women in school administration in the twentieth century. Chapter 2 provides a discussion of some of the barriers women face as they seek administrative positions. Chapter 3 provides suggestions about getting into the system, and Chapter 4 tells you how to survive once you're in the system. The final chapter provides tips on balancing your life. Since one of us is married with children, and the other is divorced with no children, we have written parts of Chapter 5 from these two different perspectives. If you desire additional reading, a list of suggested texts and sources of information is provided in the Appendix.

While we feel we have finally reached a point in our careers where we can relax a little, we realize that we have by no means arrived. The advice we offer is advice we have followed or do follow ourselves; many of the pitfalls we point out are ones in which we have from time to time found ourselves. We speak not as experts but rather as experienced travelers. Our goal is simple: to help you determine if administration is for you, to provide encouragement and guidance if it is, and to point out a few challenges you can expect on your journey to becoming a successful school administrator.

Aretha Pigford
Sandra Tonnsen

Acknowledgement

Many people have affected our lives and illuminated our paths to school administration. By doing so, they have influenced the development of this book. We acknowledge our parents, who taught us to believe in ourselves and to pursue excellence. We acknowledge our friends, who reminded us of the importance of caring for and helping others. We acknowledge our male colleagues in the educational administration program at the University of South Carolina, who have both taught us and allowed us to teach them.

This book came about as a result of our work with the Women's Institute at the University of South Carolina. The women who have participated in the institute have challenged us. They inspired the writing of this book and have contributed greatly to it through the sharing of their experiences. We are forever grateful for their strength, their honesty, and their trust.

To write a book requires considerable assistance. We are indebted to Dr. Kenneth Campbell of the University of South Carolina's College of Journalism for his expert feedback on the manuscript; to Mr. Istifanus Sanga for his technical assistance; and to Dr. Paula Baker, Ms. Laura Chastain, and Ms. Vivian Gehlken for their research assistance. We acknowledge, too, the assistance of Ms. Pat Lindler, whose skills and professionalism made our work so much easier.

1

Women: Outsiders to the Good Ol' Boy Network

From Then to Now

Women nurture learners; men run schools [1]. It's been that way for the past 100 years, and the prospect for change looks bleak. Despite the fact that women dominate America's classrooms, men still occupy the principal's office. When Ella Flagg Young was appointed the first woman superintendent of the Chicago public schools in 1909, she predicted, "In the near future we will have more women than men in executive charge of the vast educational system" [2]. Since her prediction, there has been only one period in the twentieth century when women held a majority of the principalships. In 1928, 55 percent of the elementary principalships were held by women. During that same period, however, women held less than 8 percent of the secondary school principalships and only 1.6 percent of the district superintendencies [3].

As schools enter the twenty-first century, Young's prediction remains a dream deferred. Despite the enactment of equal opportunity legislation and the Women's Liberation Movement in the 1960s, women continue to be sorely underrepresented in school administration. While women comprised almost three-fourths of America's public school teachers in 1990 [4], they held only 34 percent of the elementary principalships, 12 percent of the secondary principalships, and 5 percent of the superintendencies [5]. Women may have come a long way in some fields, but school administration is not one of them.

Determining just how far women have come can itself present a formidable challenge. Available data are often confounded, incomplete, or inconsistent. For example, while the American Association of School Administrators (AASA) reported that 8.6 percent of secondary school principalships were held by women in 1985 [6], Shakeshaft reported only 3.5 percent for that same year [7]. Prior to the report of the Equal Employment Opportunity Commission (EEOC) in 1970, there was no systematic national collection of data on women in school administration. Even the EEOC reports are often incomplete. They neither include all school districts, nor do they consistently distinguish between elementary and secondary principals and assistant principals [8]. Given these facts, the status of female school administrators may in fact be far more dismal than the numbers suggest.

Shakeshaft asserts that the absence of accurate data on women administrators is by design and is evidence of a "conspiracy of silence" [9]. Without accurate data, the status of women administrators remains blurred and ambiguous. Without facts, we are free to make whatever assumptions we choose and may feel neither a responsibility nor an obligation to act.

Today's Administrator: A Profile

Fitting the pieces of the puzzle together, we get a glimpse of what today's typical woman school principal looks like. She is likely to be white, to be in her mid to late forties, and to have taught for fifteen years. Usually the first-born or an only child, she is likely to have been reared in a two-parent home where her father was a farmer and her mother a homemaker. She is probably married to a college graduate, and they are likely to be parents. The typical woman principal holds a master's degree and is enrolled in a doctoral program [10].

While the data on women administrators is scanty, the data on black women in school administration is virtually nonexistent. So rare is the black woman administrator that Doughty laments,

"Nobody knows her name" [11]. The 1989−90 publication of the American Association of School Administrators (AASA) *Women and Minorities in School Administration* supports Doughty's assertion. While the AASA publication provides data on women and black administrators, data on black women administrators is conspicuously missing.

The little we know about black women administrators indicates that they are at the bottom of the administrative heap and are likely to hold either staff positions or positions that deal with minority concerns [12]. They generally assume their first administrative position in their mid-forties to early fifties after having taught for twelve to twenty years. Unlike white women, black women administrators are likely to come from homes where their mothers worked outside the home in unskilled labor positions. In addition, black women are more likely to be married than are white women. While white women administrators are likely to be active in professional organizations, black women devote considerable time to church activities [13]. Although black women school administrators are usually elementary principals assigned to the "so-called tough, predominantly black school[s]" [14], the expectations for their performance are extremely high. More often than not, they meet the challenge. Characterized as "warriors," black women administrators have a strong sense of mission and accomplishment and "exhibit an intensity about their work not often evident among their colleagues" [15].

The profile of the typical male principal provides a striking contrast to his female counterpart. He is likely to have spent only five years as a teacher before attaining his first administrative position and is therefore considerably younger than the typical female school administrator. In addition, the male administrator is much more likely to be married (92 percent of male principals are married compared to 59.8 percent of female principals). He is less likely to be a member of a minority and more likely to be from a small, rural community [16].

Contrasting the male and female administrator, Shakeshaft explains:

The "average" woman administrator . . . is more likely to be older, of a different race, religion, and political party, to be unmarried, and from a more urban background than her male counterpart. She is more likely to hold liberal views, to be more supportive of women's rights, and to understand the issues of single parents and divorce more personally. [17]

In some respects, male and female administrators are indeed quite different. The variables on which they differ (e.g., age, race, marital status), however, are not related to the functions of school administration and do not therefore account for the disparity in women's representation in school administration. How then does one explain the overwhelming underrepresentation of women in school administration?

Defining a Woman's Place

The times have changed, but many of the barriers confronting women have not. During the colonial period, a woman's place was clearly defined: in the home. Her role was defined equally clearly: to care for her family. The enactment of laws restricting women's rights and opportunities helped ensure that women stayed in their places and fulfilled their roles. For example, in 1903 the New York Board of Education adopted a bylaw that barred a married woman from teaching unless her husband was "mentally or physically incapacitated to earn a living or [had] deserted her for a period of not less than one year" [18].

Interestingly, however, as the needs of society changed, so did society's opposition to having married women in classrooms. During World War II, when women were needed to fill the vacancies created by men going off to war, teaching, marriage, and motherhood suddenly came to be viewed as quite compatible. Ironically, however, this change in attitude toward married women teachers resulted in an increased public sentiment against single women teachers, and school boards began to refuse to employ single women [19].

Although finally allowed to teach, women were clearly not expected to lead, despite Ella Flagg Young's assertion in 1909 that "a woman is better qualified for [school administration] than a man" [20]. The prevailing attitude was that the "natural order" dictated that men lead and women follow. In fact, teaching was viewed as a "woman's natural profession" in that it prepared women to be subordinates.

In 1915, in response to women being placed in "teaching principalships," William Chancellor argued that only men should be appointed as principals because they had a "superior executive gift" [21]. A growing body of research suggests that, if such a "gift" exists, women administrators are far more likely than men to possess it. For example, Smith reports that women principals are more skilled than men in building positive school climates, perceiving and solving problems, and facilitating positive school and community relationships [22]. Owens has found that teachers and supervisors rate women principals highly for their ability to manage school finances, handle disciplinary problems, and manage effectively [23]. Research by Hoyle indicates that women principals are perceived to be more effective than men in making decisions and in anticipating potential problem situations [24]. Findings from more than a dozen studies led Swiderski to conclude that "women administrators promote better pupil learning and better teacher performance than do male principals" [25]. Despite such findings, women still struggle to overcome the patriarchal view that the ability to be an effective leader rests with the male gender.

Keeping Women in Their Place

A variety of strategies have been used to perpetuate male dominance in school administration. One strategy that has proved to be highly effective has been to limit women's access to important networks. Historically women have been denied membership in a number of powerful professional organizations. For example, the National Teachers' Organization did not admit women until almost ten years after its founding, Phi Delta Kappa did not accept women as members until the 1970s, and the Rotary Club denied membership to women as late as 1988 [26].

Despite the obstacles they encountered, women created opportunities to exercise leadership. Some founded and led educational organizations; others began their own schools and appointed themselves as administrators. After gaining the right to vote in 1920, women used their power to elect women to administrative positions. In 1900, only 276 of the county superintendencies were held by women. In 1922, two years after women won the right to vote, women held 857 of the county superintendencies. Six years later, that number had increased to 900 [27].

Once in educational leadership positions, women found still more barriers to be overcome. Although afforded the title "principal," women administrators were afforded neither the status nor the respect given their male colleagues. The difference in salaries of male and female administrators provides irrefutable evidence of the second-class status of female administrators. In 1905 an average male elementary principal earned $1,542 while his female counterpart earned only $970 [28]. Almost eighty years later, despite the fact that women administrators have more years of teaching experience and are better educated (as evidenced by more degrees) than their male counterparts, the salaries of women administrators were 65 percent of the salaries of males in the same category. Of those principals reporting incomes over $30,000, 71 percent were men and only 29 percent were women [29].

While external barriers have certainly affected the representation of women in administration, internal barriers have also played a major role. Socialized to be followers, many women have developed self-limiting beliefs about their roles and abilities. Such beliefs have caused them to restrict their professional choices to roles viewed as "gender-appropriate."

External and internal barriers to administrative positions are not relics of the past. Both are alive and well as we prepare to enter the twenty-first century. Chapter 2 provides a discussion of some of the internal and external barriers currently faced by aspiring and practicing female school administrators.

2

Barriers to the Good Ol' Boy Network

Mary is a forty-five-year-old teacher. In the 60s she studied to become a teacher because she felt that as a young woman she had only three career choices—to be a secretary, nurse, or teacher. Her parents had taught her to study hard, be a good girl, and not think too highly of herself. ("Pride goeth before a fall.") Although she had prepared herself for a career, Mary's goal, as stated in her senior yearbook, was to "become an educated housewife." Upon graduation from college, she married her college sweetheart and began teaching to support him through law school. Now, eleven years and two children later, Mary finds herself a divorced, single parent.

After more than ten years in the classroom, she feels the need to do something different. She has talked to her principal who has encouraged her to study school administration and to become a principal herself. While the idea is exciting, Mary is hesitant; she does not know if she'd be taken seriously as a school administrator; she's not even sure she can do the job. She's had several principals who were poor managers and leaders and has often thought that she could do a better job; now that she's seriously considering a career change, she's not so sure. Mary wonders if male teachers would support a female administrator. And would she be able to maintain a friendly relationship with the teachers who are currently her colleagues?

Then, too, Mary worries about discrimination. She has read in the local newspaper that her district has an extremely low percentage of female administrators. She has never had a female principal. The only female administrator she knows is Jane W., who handles paperwork related to staff development at the district office. The district's explanation for the shortage of female school administrators is that few women have the appropriate credentials. The thought of coursework and tests intimidates her.

And what about her two young children? Would she be able to be there for them and handle the pressures of running a school at the same time? Mary knows that she is no longer satisfied with being a teacher, but these fears plague her. She is stymied by the uncertainty of it all.

Aspiring female school administrators must be adept at clearing hurdles and overcoming barriers. Some barriers may be internal, such as those concerning a woman's feelings about herself and her roles. Others will be external, such as institutional structures and practices that restrict women's access to administrative positions. Since the first step to overcoming barriers is to be aware of them, this chapter will identify some of the barriers women can expect to encounter on their way to becoming school administrators. It should be noted that many of these barriers are faced by women seeking positions of leadership in any profession.

Internal Barriers

SOCIALIZATION IN THE HOME

> "The first problem for all of us, men and women, is not to learn, but to unlearn."
>
> —Gloria Steinem [30]

Most of us go about our daily lives without thinking seriously about who we are and how we've become who we are. Were we to consider those questions, we'd realize that our perceptions of ourselves are strongly influenced—if not determined—by the things we've been taught and the experiences we've had. Those of us who have been taught to be aggressive and who have experienced power are likely to view ourselves as powerful; those who have been taught to be passive and who have experienced helplessness will tend to feel powerless.

From the moment the magical words, "It's a boy!" or "It's a girl!" are uttered, children are provided different messages and experiences based solely upon their gender. Dressed in their dainty, pink outfits, girls are treated like fragile creatures who must be protected and handled with care. In pairs or small groups, they learn to play games where everyone gets a turn, winning is not stressed, and boasting is discouraged [31]. Throughout their formative years, girls learn the importance of being polite, clean, and courteous [32].

Boys, on the other hand, are encouraged to be active, to explore, to be independent, and to take charge. They play games that have definite leaders and followers as well as clear winners and losers. Boasting and competition are not only accepted, but encouraged [33]. Through participation in group games and other team sports, boys experience competition and develop confidence early in their lives. The expectation for boys is that they will be adventuresome, get dirty, and even have a few fights [34].

SOCIALIZATION IN SCHOOLS

If by some slim chance a child enters school unable to distinguish between behaviors considered "masculine" and those considered "feminine," schools will most assuredly teach and reinforce behaviors considered to be "gender-appropriate." The very structure of elementary schools, where more than 80 percent of the teachers are women and more than 80 percent of the principals are men, sends children a clear message regarding the roles of men and women: women nurture children; men run schools [35]. Lessons on gender are continued in elementary classrooms, where boys and girls are assigned "gender-appropriate" duties and toys. Girls dust, wash paintbrushes, and do housekeeping chores, while boys collect money, run errands, and operate equipment [36]. Girls jump rope and play with dolls and tea sets while boys amuse themselves with blocks, trucks, and train sets. To be chosen the "teacher's pet," girls learn to be passive, cooperative, quiet, and conforming. Boys seeking to be the "teacher's pet," however, must achieve scholastically [37]. Boys are rewarded for achievement; girls, for being nice.

To increase the likelihood that boys and girls will engage in "gender-appropriate" behaviors, strict sanctions are used. For example, girls who climb trees or enjoy contact sports are labeled "tomboys"; boys who play with dolls or enjoy more solitary, reflective activities are branded "sissies."

WOMAN LEADER: A CONTRADICTION OF TERMS?

Whether by accident or design, the socialization of males prepares them to be leaders while the socialization of females prepares them to be helpers. Given their socialization and the fact that a leader is defined using what are generally considered "masculine" traits, women seeking positions of leadership may find themselves in a quandary. They can be either women or leaders; to be both is generally viewed as contradictory [38]. Faced with this dilemma, women seeking positions of leadership have two options:

(1) To redefine leadership to include a "feminine" perspective
(2) To be resocialized

While adding a feminine perspective to leadership is preferred, it requires both social and institutional change, a process that will take considerable time and require major shifts in attitudes. Therefore, it may be more realistic for women currently seeking leadership positions to attempt to be resocialized—i.e., to develop the skills necessary to gain entry into a "man's world." After attaining positions of leadership, however, women should then work to redefine leadership to include a "feminine" perspective so that the process of resocialization becomes unnecessary for other women.

Not surprisingly, the process of resocialization is fraught with problems. In addition to resenting having to choose between being feminine or being a leader, women who attempt to adopt "masculine" behaviors often face a no-win situation. If they conform to society's behavioral expectations for women—that is, if they are accommodating, polite, and passive—they will be rejected as leaders. If, on the other hand, the women adopt "masculine" behaviors traditionally associated with leadership—that is, if they are competitive, aggressive, and tough—they may have to deny their identity. Women may find that the cost of being at the top, in terms of their self-concept, can be extremely high [39].

Unwilling to pay such a price, many women simply choose to limit themselves to traditional roles. Others who venture into traditionally male roles develop strategies for reducing role stress. For example, many women prefer not to call attention to the fact that they are assuming roles considered contradictory. Gale reported that in a study of mixed-gender groups in which women assumed leadership, Owen found that the women tried to avoid being called "leader" [40]. They performed the role but resisted the title.

LACK OF CONFIDENCE

An obvious by-product of their socialization is women's lack of confidence in their ability to be school administrators. While men generally enter teaching with the intention of moving into administration quickly, women are less likely to express a desire to be school administrators. In fact, 51 percent of beginning male teachers expressed a desire to enter school administration. Only 9 percent of the single women, 8 percent of the married women, and 19 percent of the widowed, separated, and divorced women expressed similar aspirations [41].

Unwilling to risk negative reactions from both men and women, women who aspire to positions of leadership often keep their aspirations a secret. Fearing that they will be perceived as "pushy" if they take the initiative to apply for a position, women usually wait to be asked to do so [42]. In a recent conversation with a group of women participating in the Women's Institute, several bragged that they had never applied for a position they did not get. Rather than applauding the women's accomplishments, we were concerned that their actions conformed to the stereotype of women waiting to be "sought after" [43]. Women's unwillingness to assert themselves often indicates their fear of even being perceived as disrupting the established social order. This fear compels them to at least appear passive.

ABSENCE OF ROLE MODELS

Another reason for women's lack of confidence is the absence of sufficient role models in administrative positions. In 1990, women held only 5 percent of the superintendencies, 12 percent of the secondary principalships, and 34 percent of the elementary principalships [44]. Without the presence of a sufficient number of successful women in administrative positions, women who might aspire to such positions are likely to assume that only females who are exceptionally talented and skillful can be successful. In addition, the paucity of female administrators also leads women to question whether they will have the opportunity to attain an administrative position. If women perceive that only a select few will be permitted to enter the administrative ranks before the door of opportunity is closed, many will choose not to aspire, an action which Shakeshaft calls an effective "mental health remedy" [45]. To continue to pursue a goal to which one has no real access can be psychologically damaging.

FEAR OF REJECTION

In addition to fearing the rejection of males, who often view women leaders as threats, women who deviate from typical career paths (housewife, secretary, teacher, and nurse) sometimes fear being rejected by females who have been socialized to accept men, not women, as authority figures. With women comprising an overwhelming majority of the teaching force, such an attitude can have serious implications for the female who moves from among the ranks of her female peers to a position where she supervises them. While women have generally expected and applauded the advancement of men from the classroom to the administrative ranks, they have been less likely to do so for their female counterparts. Such attitudes seem to be changing, however. A study by Jenkins found that both female teachers and male teachers who have worked with female supervisors have favorable attitudes toward working with women [46]. The more that male and female teachers work with female administrators, the more they realize that the ability to provide leadership is unrelated to gender.

COST OF SUCCESS

While some women may be paralyzed by a fear of failure, others fear the high cost of success. Successful women must confront problems ranging from increased visibility (and therefore increased opportunities for scrutiny), to hostility from males, to resentment from females, to work overload, and finally, to increased responsibility, which could include being the designated spokesperson for women on all issues.

Women also struggle with the impact that success in the workplace might have on their personal lives. To be successful often requires one to make work a priority. This is an accepted and workable practice for men, who can generally depend on their wives to handle daily household responsibilities as well as to provide them with emotional and psychological support. Women, on the other hand, are less likely to have such a support structure and may therefore have to contend with a lack of support on the job as well as at home. While 92 percent of male principals are married, only about 59 percent of female principals are married [47].

In a national survey of practicing female principals and superintendents, we asked respondents to identify barriers they encountered as they advanced to the administrative ranks. One of the barriers cited most often was marital status. Relative to this issue, women face a no-win situation. Married women administrators responding to the survey indicated that employers questioned their ability to juggle the responsibilities of their homes and families; single women administrators indicated that employers perceived them as not being sufficiently family- or child-oriented; and divorced women administrators reported that they were perceived as having no sense of family or permanency [48]. While marital status is rarely an issue for men aspiring to administrative positions, it continues to be a major issue for married, single, and divorced women.

External Barriers

Overcoming internal barriers is a necessary but not sufficient condition for gaining access to leadership opportunities. In fact, Shakeshaft cautions women against blaming themselves and argues that external barriers are the real problem [49]. While internal barriers can be overcome with individual change, external barriers require social and institutional change — changes likely to be resisted strongly by persons already in power.

FORMAL SCREENING SYSTEM

To control who gets in and who gets promoted, organizations devise their own formal and informal screening systems. Included in the formal systems are requirements for experience and credentials such as degrees and certification. While the requirement for degrees and certification used to be a barrier for women, the number of women admitted to programs in educational administration has been increasing steadily. In fact, recent reports indicate that nationally women make up almost 50 percent of the enrollment in school administration programs [50]. Arguments that women are eliminated from administrative positions because of lack of adequate professional preparation are no longer valid.

A second excuse for the underrepresentation of women in school administration usually involves experience. In a study of employment practices and procedures, Truesdale found that advertisements for administrative positions emphasized administrative experience and required only minimal teaching experience (usually three years) [51]. For male administrators, the average number of years spent teaching is five compared to fifteen years for female administrators [52]. Ironically, the one criterion on which women would have an advantage—years of teaching experience—is devalued in the administrative selection process.

INFORMAL SCREENING SYSTEM

Despite the discriminatory nature of the formal screening system, an increasing number of women are meeting specific, formal requirements. Considerably fewer, however, are able to survive the informal screening requirement that assesses the degree to which a candidate is judged to be able to "fit in" with those in power. To state it bluntly, women continue to have major difficulty being accepted by the "good ol' boys." Women's opportunities for access to this powerful network are limited although the network could be critical to their advancement. For example, women are unable to participate in men's informal "locker room" discussions or to join some fraternal and professional organizations. It is in these informal settings that information is shared, networks are developed, and decisions are made.

Although research studies have substantiated that women administrators perform as well as or better than their male counterparts [53], women aspiring to administrative positions (especially at the high school level) still struggle to overcome the stereotype of the "man in the principal's office." As I sought my first principalship, I confronted this stereotypical view firsthand. After being interviewed by a team of persons that included teachers, parents, and district administrators, I learned that a parent had commented, "She would be perfect if she were a man." When asked to elaborate on his concerns, the parent explained that the school needed a male force, someone who could "take charge, demand respect, and whip things into shape." Much to the credit of an enlightened superintendent, I was offered the opportunity to administer this school despite the parent's concerns. There is no doubt that women still have a long way to go to convince society that the principal can, in fact, wear a skirt.

Effective Principals: More Feminine than Masculine?

Despite the masculine view of leadership, recent studies indicate that effective school administrators are likely to demonstrate an increasing number of "feminine" characteristics. For example, effective principals tend to be cooperative, people-oriented, curriculum-centered, and consensus-driven [54]. Despite the growing preference for more so-called "feminine" characteristics in approaches to school administration, however, there continues to be a blatant disparity in the number of females appointed to administrative positions. Given the facts, one can hardly argue with Shakeshaft's assertion, "The primary reason that women are not hired or promoted in administrative positions is due solely to the fact that they are female" [55].

Black Women Administrators: Their Experiences

When I, a black female, sought a principalship a few years ago, the superintendent presented me a choice of two schools. One was a predominantly white, middle-income school with an extremely high level of parental involvement; the other was a predominantly black, lower-income school with limited parental involvement. He explained that the former school had never had a black principal and that the latter had never had a female principal. His question to me was: "Which do you want to deal with? Race or gender?"

Black women aspiring to administrative positions face the dual barriers of race and gender. As such, many find themselves in situations where they are confronted with both racism and sexism. The underrepresentation of black female administrators suggests either that few women have been willing to take on this challenge or that few have been provided the opportunity to do so. As already noted, Doughty describes the black female school administrator as "invisible" and laments, "Nobody knows her name" [56].

Although black women and white women face some of the same

barriers in their advancement to positions of leadership, their experiences necessarily differ. Like their white counterparts, black women must overcome internal barriers. However, given the fact that society socializes them to be second-class citizens because of both race and gender, overcoming some of the internal barriers might present a more formidable challenge.

In many cases, however, the system designed to oppress black women has in fact served as the catalyst for many to excel. In an effort to cope and survive, black women have had to develop skills that often make resocialization unnecessary for them. Black women who have served as heads of households, for example, have not had the option of serving in the role of helper, the role for which women are typically socialized. Many of their personal situations have forced them into positions of leadership early in their lives. Lightfoot reports that young black girls traditionally have assumed more family responsibilities at an earlier age than middle-class white girls and are likely to be ''more competent, more aggressive, and more adept at organization'' [57].

For the past four years, the Women's Institute has provided us opportunities to observe and analyze the behavior of black and white, prospective and newly appointed female school administrators. In one of the activities, participants are placed in groups of not more than five. All groups but two are mixed in terms of race, age, position, etc. In one group, there is a lone black female; in the other, there is a lone white female. All groups are asked to spend twenty minutes solving a problem. During the twenty-minute period, we observe the interactions of all groups, paying particular attention to the two groups in which there is a lone black or white woman. After the activity, we ask if anyone felt different in her group. Invariably, the lone white woman and the lone black woman identify themselves. We then discuss how they felt and how their feelings affected their participation. More often than not, the black woman recognizes herself as different and then participates in the assigned activity. The white woman also recognizes that she is different, but she tends to withdraw from participation. Because black women are so used to functioning as a minority, they seem to have developed skills that enable them to concentrate on the task. On the other hand, being a racial minority is such a rare experience for white women that they have not developed coping skills and seem unable to concentrate on the task.

In addition to overcoming barriers already identified, black women often struggle with a multitude of other issues as well. Those who identify with the gender struggle often fear being perceived as having lost their racial identity or having misplaced priorities. If they compete with black males for administrative positions, they may fear being accused of contributing to society's denigration of black men. While black women aspiring to administrative positions may be guilty of nothing except being ambitious, they must nevertheless be prepared for a multitude of charges that may be hurled against them.

The impact that being a school administrator can have on personal relationships may also be different for black women. Given the fact that few black men have gained the status of white men in society, black women who advance to administrative positions may stand to lose more in their personal relationships than white women. For example, black women who are unmarried will find the pool of eligible black professional men extremely small if they seek to marry someone at the same educational, professional, and income level. In addition, those who are married are likely to earn more than their spouses. Finding a husband or maintaining a relationship with a man who earns less than the woman can still be problematic.

While there is no question that women in administration carry a heavy load, black women in administration sometimes struggle with what seems to be an impossible one. The following chapter, however, offers suggestions that we hope will be helpful to women of all races.

3

Breaking into the Good Ol' Boy Network

Steffanie is a thirty-two-year-old middle school teacher. Her friends and colleagues consider her successful. She's taught for seven years. She has two bright, happy children and a husband who is a high school teacher and coach. Steffanie has just completed her master's degree in school administration. She has applied for two assistant principalship positions in neighboring school districts. Her application to the first district was promptly dismissed with a letter saying the position had already been filled. She received a preliminary interview in the second district, but felt very uncomfortable. The male interviewer wore a casual shirt and pants with loafers, and she feared the new black, tailored suit she had worn was much too formal. She felt that she had come across as too dogmatic.

Though intimidated by her first two attempts, Steffanie wants to apply again for an assistant principalship. A review of the job vacancy announcements in the local paper piques her interest. An assistant principal is needed at a middle school in another district within driving distance of her home. Steffanie knows she can do the job if she can just get past the interview. She decides to analyze her first two attempts. After carefully reviewing her resume and previous applications, she remembers an old friend who is now an administrator in the district where a vacancy currently exists. Steffanie realizes that she has never taken advantage of her friend's offers of assistance. She admits that more experienced teachers have helped her become a successful teacher. She decides that advice and assistance from a mentor in an administrative position may be equally important. She reaches for the phone.

Make no mistake about it, there is a place for you in school administration! Your challenge is to find it! To do so, you must know yourself—your needs, strengths, and weaknesses. You must know the sacrifices that are necessary, and decide if you are willing to make them. You must also know the job market—what jobs are available, where they are, and which ones will move you closer to your ultimate career goal. Once you have identified the position that you hope to claim, you have to figure out how to go about claiming it. This chapter provides a few hints that will help you meet the challenge of finding your place in the administrative ranks and then claiming it.

Know Yourself

Who are you, what do you want, and why do you want it? If you are the typical woman seeking an administrative position, you are a classroom teacher who's been teaching about fifteen years, and you're in your mid to late forties. You hold a master's degree and are probably enrolled in an educational administration program. It's likely that you're married and have held many positions of leadership in your school, church, and community.

Some of you may not fit this description. You may be younger or older, single, or relatively new to the teaching profession. Whether you are typical or not, if you think you have the potential to be a school administrator, we encourage you to go for it.

WHAT'S DRIVING YOU?

If you are to be a successful school administrator, it is important to focus not only on what you want but also on why you want it. Like many teachers, you may be suffering from classroom burnout and be considering a career change, but you aren't quite sure if administration is the route you need to travel. That's probably why you're reading this book. Before you decide if administration is for you, however, it's important to understand why you want to be a school administrator.

Are you considering school administration primarily because you have grown tired of students or because you dislike teaching? We certainly hope not. Although administrators do not deal with students in classroom settings, they continue to work with students on a regular basis. Being an administrator in no way decreases one's responsibility for children. In fact, the position of administrator does just the opposite. If you're tired of students, avoid administration. Working with children is what administration is all about.

Do you dislike teaching? If you're considering administration because you see it as an opportunity to avoid teaching, you might want to think again. Effective administrators are in fact teachers. This is particularly true of administrators who are instructional leaders. The major difference between the students of classroom teachers and the students of administrators is their age. Classroom teachers work with children; administrators work with adults who, based upon our experiences, can be much more challenging and difficult.

Recently in a mock interview for an administrative position, a female interviewee was asked why she wanted to leave teaching to become an administrator. She said, "There's too much paperwork with teaching." Having been both a teacher and a school administrator myself, I groaned. First of all, the response was inappropriate; I would never hire anyone on that basis. Secondly, the interviewee was wrong! Administration—especially with today's emphasis on accountability—involves a tremendous amount of paperwork.

ASSESS YOUR SKILLS

Perhaps you are considering school administration because you feel you have skills that can be better used in an administrative position. If so, what are those skills? Please keep in mind that skills needed in administration may differ from those needed in the classroom. In other words, do not assume that because you are an effective teacher, you will be an effective administrator. While administrators and teachers operate in similar environments, their worlds are indeed miles apart.

How comfortable are you when interacting with adults? With parents? How do you feel when conflict arises? How do you respond to pressure? To criticism? What about your communication skills? Can you express yourself orally? In writing? What about paperwork? Does it drive you crazy, or do you have a system for dealing with paper overload? What about a sense of humor? Do you have one? Can you laugh at yourself? Are you a leader? Can you get others to follow you? Can you keep them with you? Are you a good listener? Do you exude confidence? Do you present a professional image?

The ability to identify one's strengths and weaknesses is one of the skills of an effective leader. We therefore urge you to take inventory of yourself. Remember that if you want an administrative position, you need to be able to sell yourself. You must therefore know the product—*you!* Figure 1 presents an activity that should help you get to know yourself better.

After you have completed the inventory, go back over the list and place an X beside those areas you've circled that you still need to improve. Your X's in addition to the uncircled items are areas that you should incorporate in an improvement plan.

We have found that an improvement plan can lead to tremendous growth. At the end of the Women's Institute, we work with participants to analyze their strengths and weaknesses and to develop an improvement plan. Their goals range from personal ones ("I will lose 10 pounds by January 1") to professional ones ("I will make more effective oral presentations"). Figure 2 shows a sample of an improvement plan.

In our experience, the most effective plans are those that are written down; therefore, we encourage you to look back over the leadership potential inventory (Figure 1) and develop an improvement plan for yourself.

ASSESS THE COSTS

After you have an understanding of your motives, skills, and abilities, you can concentrate on whether you're willing to pay the

Circle the statements which describe you:

1. I like to learn new things.
2. I anticipate challenges.
3. I am organized.
4. I speak well in one-on-one situations.
5. I speak well to large groups.
6. I write clearly.
7. I like children.
8. I work well with both children and adults.
9. I can share power.
10. I can move from one task to another quickly.
11. I can take criticism.
12. I can provide positive feedback.
13. I can help people improve.
14. I have lots of enegry.
15. I usually make the right decisions.
16. I can make decisions without knowing all the facts.
17. I am interested in many different things.
18. I can earn the respect of both males and females.
19. I enjoy hard work.
20. I have self-confidence.
21. I can deal with conflict.
22. I can deal with ambiguity.
23. I can handle paperwork.
24. I have a sense of humor.
25. I am a good listener.

Figure 1. Leadership potential inventory.

price of school administration. Most people who make it to the top of the administrative ladder have put their careers first at some point in their lives. Since being a school administrator usually requires a greater commitment of time and energy than being a teacher, you will have less time and energy for family, friends, civic and social events, and for yourself.

If you are married, your spouse's support can be critical. If

Objectives	Activities Evaluation	Evaluation
1. Improve oral presentation skills.	A. Critique video. B. Have two individuals with good presentation skills to critique video and provide feedback. C. Make one presentation to an adult audience with "coach" present and obtain feedback. D. Read at least three articles on oral presentations. E. Critique at least two adult presenters. F. Videotape and critique oral presentation.	Compare critiques of initial video vs. final video.

Figure 2. Sample improvement plan.

there are children, you will have to juggle their needs with the demands of your job. If you do not have children but plan to, you must decide on the best time to have them—before you begin an administrative career, or while you are an administrator? If you decide to have children while you are in an administrative position, what impact will your pregnancy and the birth of your child(ren) have on your career?

What about those of you who might be single or divorced? While your marital status might allow you more time to concentrate on your career, you must still plan time for yourself, your friends, and social activities. If your friends are not supportive or understanding of your career goals, you may encounter some of the same problems a woman with an unsupportive husband faces.

Whether married, single, divorced, or widowed, you must decide whether you are willing to relocate for a job. If you are, to what locations are you willing to go? While mobility will increase your chances of obtaining an administrative position, personal preference, family situations, and/or economic realities may restrict or prohibit such ventures. In the traditional family, relocating has been done almost solely for the professional advancement of the husband. Wives have been expected to give up their jobs and provide whatever support the family needed to facilitate the husband's career advancement. Unfortunately, many husbands have not been prepared psychologically to offer the same kind of support and assistance to wives who need to relocate in order to advance in their careers.

Know the Job Market

There are many different administrative positions in education. Know what's available and where the jobs can lead you. Some positions such as principal and assistant superintendent reflect the traditional path to the superintendency. Other positions such as curriculum coordinator or personnel specialist—known as staff positions—offer support services with little authority over others. Your task will be to decide which job is best for you. Of course, your decision will be influenced by what you know about yourself, your ultimate goal, and by job availability.

GET ON THE RIGHT PATH

If you want to become a principal or superintendent, you will want to get some "line" experience, starting possibly at the assistant principalship and moving to the principalship. If you're interested in becoming a superintendent, the secondary principalship appears to be the better choice. To date, however, few women have been chosen as high school principals.

While staff positions do not typically lead to principalships, there are some staff positions you might consider: recruiter, program director or consultant, and public relations coordinator. You should be aware, however, that women already hold many of these staff positions and many of them are trapped in the same kinds of jobs women have typically held—jobs that allow them to support the decision maker without being the decision maker. The key is to be selective. Get experience where you can, but don't become "stuck."

FIND OUT WHAT'S AVAILABLE

You can't apply for a job if you don't know it's available. How do you find out about administrative vacancies? In many school systems, it is customary to send a job vacancy announcement to individual schools within the system before the vacancy is advertised elsewhere. If this is your district's practice, ask your supervisor to post all vacancy announcements, and then read the bulletin board faithfully. It is also wise to have others on the lookout for job possibilities for you. This person-to-person contact (frequently called "networking") can be extremely helpful, even crucial.

Other sources of information about job vacancies include classified advertisements in local newspapers and professional journals and newsletters. For example, *Education Week* provides an extensive listing of administrative vacancies on a regular basis. In addition to reading journals that have general circulation, black women should also read newspapers, journals, and newsletters that target black readers. Women should also review newsletters and flyers of state school administrator organizations. Our state school administrator association operates a job vacancy hotline. Calling the hotline number gives the association member free access to listings of administrative vacancies within the state. The key, of course, is to be a member of such organizations so that you can have access to their services.

DO YOUR HOMEWORK

Once you have identified a position that interests you, find out as much as you can about the position. Talk to people who know the expectations of the job. Read the job description. If the position is in a district other than your own, conduct an investigation of the district, the job itself, and the community. Read the district's recruitment brochures, but go beyond that. State education agencies can usually provide demographic, academic, and financial information about individual school districts. Minutes from board meetings and financial statements are usually public information, and can shed light on the philosophy and politics of the school district.

It's important, too, that you be familiar with cutting-edge practices. Recently one of my students, a high school assistant principal, sought a middle school position in a progressive district. She asked for advice and I suggested that she read *Turning Points,* a recent publication on the middle school concept. She did, and reported that while none of the interview questions were specific to *Turning Points,* her knowledge of middle school philosophy was questioned. She reported that the interviewer seemed to be impressed when she cited specific ideas from *Turning Points.* She got the job!

Prepare Yourself

In the past, if you were a white male coach with at least two years of teaching experience, it was probable that you would be promoted to an administrative position—frequently the high school principalship. This has not been and is not presently the case for women. The competition for most administrative jobs is fierce. More and more people are earning degrees in school administration and becoming certified in administrative areas. When preparing for an administrative position, remember the three C's: Contacts, Competence, and Confidence.

CONTACTS

Knowing the right people is still one of the quickest ways to career advancement. For women in particular, having contacts or mentors can be critical. Carr-Ruffino defines a mentor as "a more experienced person at a higher level in your organization who takes a promising younger person under his or her wing as a protege" [58].

Mentors serve a variety of functions. They provide support, feedback, and honest appraisal. They advise you of potential job vacancies. They serve as role models. They introduce you to the "right" people. It is important to have both male and female mentors if possible. Usually, the male mentor has more power and other contacts up the administrative ladder. Female mentors, on the other hand, can offer empathy, support, and advice from a woman's point of view.

Because of a dearth of black women administrators, black women aspiring to administrative positions are unlikely to find black women mentors. While having a mentor of the same race and gender may be preferred, it is not necessary. The important point is to utilize the best available source for gaining entry into the administrative ranks. White men are generally in the best position to provide that entry.

Carr-Ruffino [59] states that a mentor can:

- teach, advise, counsel, coach, guide, and sponsor
- give insights into the business
- serve as a sounding board for decision making
- be a constructive critic
- provide necessary information for career advancement
- show the protege how to move effectively through the system
- help the protege cut through red tape
- teach the protege the "political ropes" and introduce him/her to the right people

- stand up for the protege in meetings or discussions with his or her peers; in cases of controversy, fight for the protege
- suggest the protege as a likely candidate when appropriate opportunities come along
- increase the protege's visibility; single him/her out from the crowd of competitors surrounding him/her and argue his/her virtues against theirs
- provide an important signal to other people that the protege has his/her backing; help to provide the protege with an aura of power and upward mobility

This list makes the importance of a mentor very clear. It also points out the characteristics you will want in seeking a mentor. Only an intelligent, honest, respected individual who is either at the top of the administrative hierarchy or is on his or her way there can provide most of these supports.

Finding appropriate mentors is not always easy. Formal internships or mentorships are convenient ways to establish a mentoring relationship, but they are not always available. To identify possible mentors, you should attend meetings of administrative organizations, talk to both men and women who have "made it," seek advice from your college professors in administration, and increase your visibility in as many positive ways as possible.

A successful mentor relationship is probably more a function of chemistry than of anything else. Find someone you like and who likes and respects you. Then use that person's knowledge, skills, and professional relationships to learn as much as you can about school administration.

COMPETENCE

Although few would deny that "connections" are important in career advancement, most of us still prefer to be hired because of our knowledge and skills. Competence begins with appropriate training and certification. If the current trend continues, women who enter their first administrative positions will have more training (i.e., courses and degrees) than their male counterparts. This is particularly true of women administrators at the secondary level.

Get the Credentials

If you do not hold administrative certification, enroll in a degree program in school administration. Many colleges and universities offer one or more degrees in educational administration: master's, educational specialist, and doctorate (either a doctor of philosophy or doctor of education). In many states, administrator certification is tied to completion of a graduate program in administration. For example, a master's degree in administration may be required for principal certification. In any case, contact your state department of education or the agency that offers administrative certification and find out what you need.

If you need to return to school, recognize the positive benefits that await you. You not only learn basic administrative principles, theories, and skills, you also have the opportunity to make contacts with people who might be able to facilitate your career. In one of our recent classes, there were five district personnel directors. Also, both of us moved into the professorate and university administration through contacts with our professors. As professors ourselves, we have helped other women obtain administrative positions.

Make Yourself Known

Once you have obtained the necessary credentials, seek opportunities to demonstrate your skills. Find out if your school district sponsors any type of internship or apprenticeship program. If it does, apply to participate. If such programs are not available, ask for administrative duties at your current school and volunteer to serve on district committees. Get yourself known.

One of the reasons coaches move quickly into administrative positions is their visibility. You've got to be seen by those who are in positions to promote you. Women tend to feel that if they do an outstanding job in their classrooms, their skills will be recognized and they will be promoted to an administrative position, if they desire it. It is true that you do need a record of excellent performance, but that performance must be in highly visible areas. Classrooms are notorious for isolation and low visibility. What you need to do is to assume responsibilities outside the classroom that put you in the spotlight. Once you have center stage, demonstrate what you can do.

We encourage you, too, to seek assistance provided specifically to women. While you must possess many of the same skills required of male administrators, you must also develop skills that help you deal with gender-related issues. Courses, workshops, and books designed specifically for the female prospective administrator can be particularly helpful. Examples of the few that are available are provided in the Appendix.

CONFIDENCE

Successful administrators have to exude confidence—even if they're only faking it! Confidence is a balanced sense of self. It's knowing that you can handle most situations and knowing when to get help if you can't. It's knowing you're not better or worse than other administrators—that, like others, you have certain strengths and weaknesses.

Confident people are neither cocky nor self-effacing. They know themselves and convey to others their self-assuredness through their posture, their poise, their speech. They dress with a flair that says, "I know who I am and I'm proud of me." And they do it without affronting others.

If you need a confidence booster, sit down and list your accomplishments over the past six months or year. You'll be pleasantly surprised. Learn from your failures, then forget them. But never, ever forget a single success.

Implement Successful Job-Hunting Strategies

MARKET YOURSELF ON PAPER

A successful job hunt begins with the development of a resume. A resume should be a brief but comprehensive compendium of your accomplishments. Rather than a simple listing of degrees and past jobs, the resume should detail the responsibilities you've had, especially those that have required supervisory skills. It should be well organized, with the most important information on the first page, easily accessible to the prospective employer. There should be absolutely no errors on a resume since it is likely to be viewed as your best effort.

Remember that your resume communicates the very first impression of you. Make it a good one. Be sure to use letter-quality type and have your resume printed on high-quality, soft cream or gray paper.

A letter of interest or a letter of application should accompany the resume (see Figure 3). The letter should briefly summarize your qualifications for the job. Generally, three paragraphs on a single page are enough, as follows:

- paragraph one: expression of interest in a particular job
- paragraph two: summary of qualifications
- paragraph three: expression of thanks with information for follow-up

For many positions, you may be asked to complete an application form. There are several rules that should be followed when completing the application:

(1) Always be honest.
(2) Fill in every space, using NA (not applicable) when necessary.
(3) Make no errors.
(4) Be neat.
(5) Leave no unexplained gaps in your employment history.

MARKET YOURSELF IN PERSON

The next step in the employment process is typically the interview. When you receive the call to schedule your interview, try to find out as much as you can. For example, it's advantageous to know

Date

Name of Person, Institution
Address
Address
City, State, Zip Code

Dr. Jane Doe
Assistant Superintendent for Personnel
Right On School District
Best, Minnesota

Dear Dr. Doe:

   Please accept this letter as my application for the assistant principalship at Bestever High School. My resume is enclosed.

   I feel that I am well qualified for the position. I have a bachelor's degree in English and a master's degree in School Administration. I have been an English teacher for the past five years. During this time, I have had the opportunity to assume additional responsibilities. I facilitated the District Discipline Committee and was chairperson of the district's English Curriculum Committee. For the past two years, I have served on the superintendent's Advisory Committee.

   Thank you for your consideration. I can be reached at 444-0000.

Sincerely,

Ima Winner

Figure 3. Sample cover letter for application.

who is conducting the interview. While many personnel specialists still prefer the one-on-one interview, it is becoming increasingly common to see an interview team of four to ten people. A word of advice here. Apply for every job in which you are interested and for which you are qualified; however, don't expect to be invited for an interview each time you apply. Whether you are interviewed or not may have nothing to do with your application or qualifications. Many employment decisions are political. If, after a reasonable length of time, you have not been informed of your status as an applicant, we would encourage you to contact the personnel office for information.

Let's assume that you are invited for an interview. You should plan carefully and thoroughly for the interview, remembering that there are two purposes to any job interview:

(1) To help you determine if you want to work in that school or district
(2) To help the interviewer decide if you're the best person for the job

Remember, too, that an interview is not adversarial. Assume that the person interviewing you wants you to succeed.

We need to caution you here. Some of your interviews will be polished and professional. Others, disappointingly, may be cursory, ill-planned, and poorly executed. Women and blacks often complain that they are asked to interview for positions for which they are not being seriously considered. In our opinion, their complaint is well founded. In an effort to meet affirmative action guidelines for personnel selection, women and blacks are often interviewed merely to enable the district to go through the motions. Our advice is to do your best in each situation and learn from it. Remember, the more practice you have in actual interview situations, the more skilled you become. This is not to say, however, that you should always accept being a "token" interviewee. Sometimes it is necessary to fight for a position. If you feel that your rights have been violated in the selection process, you can file a grievance or take legal action. Before doing so, however, you need to weigh the pros and cons in light of the impact such action might have on your professional relationships. We're sure you've heard the adage, "You only get one chance to make a good first impression." That first impression with an interviewer is crucial. As a matter of fact, in a recent study, it was found that 70 percent of the responding interviewers made critical judgments about the interviewee within the *first three minutes* of the interview [60].

There are several preliminary steps that you should take to prepare for the interview:

(1) Find out everything you can about the vacancy, the school, and the district. Read the district's brochures, study its financial statement, read the job description, talk to someone in the district or school who can give you useful background information, preferably a friend, or a friend of a friend. Know the cutting-edge concepts in the area in which you're interviewing.

(2) Anticipate some of the questions you will likely be asked during the interview and plan your responses. Some typical questions are:
- Tell me a little bit about yourself.
- Why did you choose a career in education?
- Why do you want to be an administrator?
- Why do you want to work in this district/school?
- What are your strengths? Weaknesses?
- What do you plan to be doing five years from now?
- Why should we hire you?

(3) Practice interviewing. Get someone to conduct a mock interview with you. Have the interview videotaped. Then review the tape to see what you can do to improve. Practice until you feel comfortable and like what you see on the video.

(4) Plan what you're going to wear to the interview. A navy or other appropriate dark suit is a must for every female administrative aspirant. The right suit is flattering on just about everyone. It's polished, conservative, and makes the right personal and professional statement about you. Your outfit should enhance your professional image. It should be something in which you're comfortable. It's generally not a good idea to wear a new outfit to an interview. Be careful that nothing you wear—your jewelry, your perfume, your hair-

style—detracts from the professional statement you wish to make.
(5) Find out the exact location of the interview and allow plenty of time to get there. Plan to arrive at least ten minutes early, allowing yourself some time to relax and to check your appearance.

The planning and preparation that you do prior to the interview will give you additional confidence as you begin the interview. Enter the interview room with an air of confidence. Smile, shake hands, make eye contact with those who will be interviewing you. Check your posture. You want to appear poised and confident even though you may not be.

The interviewer will probably start the interview with some small talk. Get involved in that small talk. It should help you relax and feel more confident.

During the interview itself, there are several things that you should do. First of all, listen very, very carefully to the questions. If you don't understand the question, say so. If you don't know the answer, say so. Answer each question as honestly and openly as possible. Don't ramble—just answer the question. If you need time to think through an answer, take that time. Don't be afraid of silence. A thoughtful interviewee makes a better impression than a "shoot-from-the-hip" one. Don't be afraid of a little humor. You certainly don't want to come across as the class clown, but it's perfectly acceptable to laugh at yourself. You want the interviewer to see the human side of you.

During the interview, make frequent eye contact with the interviewer(s). Looking at the interviewers helps you to appear honest, open, interested, and confident. Generally, it's better to keep your hands open and in sight. Keep them on your lap if there is no table directly in front of you. When there is a table, you can keep your hands open on it.

Gestures with your hands and facial expressions should be relatively tame, but they should not be eliminated. You want to come across as natural and vibrant. We recently witnessed an interview where the female interviewee sent mixed messages to the interviewers. She talked about how enthusiastic she was about a certain program yet neither her voice nor her gestures indicated any enthusiasm or excitement.

Don't be surprised by the typical final question, "What questions do you have for me?" Make sure you have one or two well-thought-out, appropriate questions. Use the information you gathered earlier to design thoughtful questions that are relatively easy for the interviewer to answer. One question that we like is, "What are you proudest of in this school/district?"

Conclude the interview with a handshake and a "thank you." Try to find out the next steps in the procedure so that you can make other job-seeking plans. It is appropriate to write a thank-you note to the interviewer. The note, however, should be brief, basically saying thanks and reemphasizing your interest in the position.

Conclusion

As with any written document, the advice in this chapter appears to be one-dimensional and sequential. In real life, things don't happen that way. Things will occur simultaneously; they'll occur out of order, or they won't occur at all. You may have to have many interviews before you land an administrative position. You may be offered an administrative position before you think you're ready. If you know yourself, however, if you know the kind of position you want, and if you take the steps outlined above, your chances for getting the opportunity to be a school administrator should be enhanced.

4

Prospering in the Good Ol' Boy Network

When she became principal of Topnotch School, Janie heard that her male predecessor was "tough" and "ran a tight ship." Although she could be tough when necessary, she preferred a more gentle, nonthreatening leadership style. Unlike her predecessor, she wanted her staff to respect—not fear—her.

At the very first staff meeting, Janie made it clear she would have an open-door policy and invited her staff to interact with her freely on any issue. As the year progressed, more and more teachers accepted her invitation. At first, she was pleased that teachers were opening up to her, but later began to notice that most of the issues they wanted to discuss were personal, not professional. She was learning far more than she wanted to know about sick children and relatives, divorce proceedings, wayward children, and problem relationships. Janie also noted that the conversations tended to end with teachers asking for special favors (e.g., to leave school early, to have a special teaching assignment, etc.). While Janie wants to be sympathetic, she feels she must guard against being taken advantage of. Some of the teachers are beginning to say that she is "too soft" and she's also noticed that teacher attendance is declining. She fears that a decline in student achievement will follow. As she walks into her office, she wonders if the time has arrived when she should close her door.

Now that you have finally achieved your goal of becoming a school administrator, there will be days when you may ask yourself, "What am I doing here?" "What have I gotten myself into?" Stop and remind yourself that you have worked very hard to get where you are, that you have prepared yourself well, and that you're in an ideal position to help students. You can do it! With those thoughts in mind, the tips that follow should help you survive and prosper as an educational leader.

First, remember the intricate complexities involved in female leadership. Edith Lynch reminds us that

> In addition to the ability to do a good job, a female executive must be extremely flexible, have a sense of humor, be completely unabashed by male ego, and not take herself too seriously.
>
> She must carry her load of work and then some. She must be a female. She must be patient, polite, sympathetic, and understanding and at the same time be very decisive. She must always maintain a coolness, dignity, and aloofness, while still being warm and friendly. [61]

To be an effective leader, you must focus on people and the task. In addition to these dimensions, however, there is an equally important dimension that we'll call the "self" dimension. Because women are likely to be more concerned about others than about themselves, the "self" dimension becomes very important. Concern for self means being aware of the impact of one's self on the organization and the reciprocal impact of the organization on the individual. Figure 4 represents our attempt to categorize behaviors for each dimension. In this chapter, we will discuss both the human and task dimensions. The self dimension will be explored in Chapter 5.

Building and Maintaining Interpersonal Relations

To be a successful leader in any organization, you must work well with and through people. Education is a "people" profession and women tend to be people-oriented. If you are the typical female administrator, your style is "cooperative" and you see yourself not as a boss, but rather as an "empowerer" of others [62]. Because of your style, you are able to work with people at all levels: school boards, colleagues, teachers, parents, classified staff, the business

Human Dimension	Task Dimension	Self Dimension
• Building and maintaining interpersonal relations	• Managing time • Communicating • Dealing with subordinates	• Keeping current • Presenting a professional image • Managing stress • Balancing your life

Figure 4. Dimensions of leadership.

community, etc. In some of these dealings you will be the superordinate; in others, the subordinate. In some you will be the public servant; in others, the friend and confidante. Because women are so accustomed to assuming a variety of roles, you are probably quite adept at moving from one role to another with grace and skill.

Unlike your male colleagues, it is more likely that you tend to emphasize relationships and are accustomed to communicating with people at all levels — the educated as well as the uneducated. You are also likely to have "sensing skills" that enable you to pick up on nonverbal cues and to understand others' feelings and reactions [63]. In addition to these skills, however, it is also important that you develop a reputation for being honest and trustworthy. You can do so by being truthful, keeping confidences, and refraining from gossip.

We hope you laugh easily. Otherwise, your days as an administrator are numbered. No matter how frustrated you might become, how hopeless things may seem, or how overworked you may feel, find something to chuckle about every day. A sense of humor, the ability to take things lightly, the ability to laugh at yourself (particularly when others laugh at you) not only facilitates positive interpersonal relations but also minimizes your own personal stress.

A recent incident reminded me of the importance of being able to laugh at oneself. I was team teaching the principalship class to a group of graduate students. Two other professors — both male — were sitting in the class while I lectured. Immediately before class began,

I had gulped down a soft drink. In the middle of a sentence, a loud, uncontrollable burp slipped out. I was mortified! But, there was absolutely nothing I could do about it. I laughed, the students laughed, and so did my two colleagues. After the comic relief, I regained my composure, apologized, and continued my dialogue with the students. Will my students remember the incident? Probably. Will they think less of me as a professor or a person? Probably not. My sense is that they see me as more human.

Managing Time

We all experience time crunches when there just do not seem to be enough hours in the day. We work long hours. We work weekends. Such a schedule might be necessary at times. More frequently, however, it is the result of poor time management. While managing one's time is important for any school administrator, for the female school administrator — who is likely attempting to balance home and career responsibilities — time management is critical.

One of the first steps in managing time is to be sure that you're not confusing being busy with being productive. With all that will be expected of you, we can assure you that you can be busy every minute of the day. But "busyness" does not necessarily mean that you're being productive. Posner explains, "The executive is judged by what he accomplishes, not by how many hours he puts in" [64]. Productive administrators decide what activities are important, develop a plan for completing them, and — more often than not — they complete them. If you don't get in the habit of planning your day, be assured that there will be lots of people waiting to do it for you.

Expecting an administrator to always adhere to a planned schedule is unrealistic. There will be times when unexpected events will demand your time and attention. However, those times should be the exception — not the rule. What are some strategies that can help you maximize your use of time? To understand how you currently spend your time, keep a time log of the activities you perform for several days. On a sheet of paper, simply record each activity and the time devoted to it. At the end of each day, analyze the log to determine if the tasks were essential to the accomplishment of your goals. What was unnecessary? Was the unnecessary activity avoidable? What could you have done to save time? After several days of such analysis, you should be able to make some adjustments to maximize your use of time. If you find, however, that you simply have too much to do, you may need to persuade your superiors that you need extra help or fewer assignments.

Then, too, you may be having trouble distinguishing between what is urgent and what is important. Posner quotes Hummel as he reminds us of the difference: "We live in constant tension between the urgent and the important. The problem is that the important tasks rarely must be done today, or even this week. The urgent task calls for instant action—endless demands pressure every hour and day" [65].

As you analyze your time log, note the number of times you move from one matter to another. Do you give the important tasks (i.e., those that help you achieve organizational and personal goals) their due? Without deliberate planning, an administrator is likely to move from one fire to the next, and to deal with one piece of "administrivia" after the other. Such action, however, may enhance your management skills at the expense of your much-needed leadership. To be a leader, you must concentrate on the big picture, that is, the *important* tasks.

Of the top ten time wasters identified by Mackenzie [66], which do you need to address?

(1) Telephone interruptions
(2) Drop-in visitors
(3) Ineffective delegation
(4) Meetings
(5) Lack of objectives, priorities, planning
(6) Crisis management
(7) Attempting too much at once

(8) Cluttered desk/personal disorganization
(9) Indecision/procrastination
(10) Inability to say "no"

Following is a discussion of techniques you might use to address each of these time wasters.

TELEPHONE INTERRUPTIONS

The key to handling telephone interruptions is an efficient, knowledgeable, sensitive secretary who will politely screen your calls, help callers when possible, refer them to others as appropriate, and help you establish a call-back block of time. This call-back period allows you to control your time. You decide when you'll talk on the phone and, to some degree, how long you'll talk. You can block out a period of time to return calls when you know the other party won't be interested in talking too long (i.e., right before the lunch hour or right before the end of the workday). While you should control the timing of your telephone conversations, you should never fail to return phone calls in a timely fashion.

DROP-IN VISITORS

As a school administrator you realize that parents and students will often drop in to visit. While it is important that you be accessible, parents and students should be encouraged to schedule visits with you whenever possible. Because women tend to value relationships, they are likely to embrace an "open-door policy." That's fine. It is important to point out, however, that such a policy does not mean that one's door must be open literally. It merely implies that one is willing to be accessible and available. If you're going to be effective, you're going to have to be willing to close your door from time to time and focus on whatever task is before you. Don't feel guilty. We can assure you that a closed door will not prevent you from being informed of any major problem that might arise. Looking back on our days as administrators, we realize that there were many days when we should have closed our office doors, kicked our heels off, read a good journal, and just relaxed.

There are a number of strategies that can help you minimize the need for unscheduled visits. As you walk through the school building, keep a pad and pen with you at all times. This encourages faculty and staff to visit with you as you "manage by wandering around" [67]. When they see you in the classrooms, halls, or lounge, they can tell you what's on their minds. If they need to see you privately, they can schedule an appointment, thereby helping you gain control over your own time.

Vendors may be important to the success of certain school activities, but your secretary should provide them access to you only when they have an appointment and when you are the appropriate person with whom they need to speak. For example, a vendor selling carpet cleaning supplies should be directed to the building supervisor — not the principal. Also, if you are not interested in the product or service being offered, have your secretary communicate this fact to the vendor and refuse to see him or her.

At those infrequent times when you do decide to entertain drop-in visitors, there are some techniques you can employ to minimize the length of the visit. For example, you might

(1) Remain standing
(2) Not offer the visitor a seat
(3) Not offer refreshments
(4) Arrange with your secretary in advance a method for her to extract you graciously from the visit

INEFFECTIVE DELEGATION

One of the keys to effective delegation is knowledge of the strengths and weaknesses of your faculty and staff. Take time at the beginning of your new job to talk to your staff. Find out what their jobs are, what they like and dislike about their jobs and the organization, and what their aspirations are. Posner [68] offers ten guidelines for effective delegation.

(1) Find the right person to do the job.
(2) Make sure that he/she has the proper equipment, supplies, supports, etc., to do the job effectively.
(3) Trust the person.
(4) Be aware of reverse delegation, for example, the teacher who says to you, "We have a problem."
(5) Accept responsibility for the work you've delegated.
(6) Follow up to make sure he/she understands what's to be done.
(7) Leave the person as much freedom as possible to complete the task.
(8) Be selective in what you delegate.
(9) Delegate in advance. Don't drop the report that's due tomorrow on your assistant's desk at 3 P.M. today.
(10) Delegate more than the dull and the dirty. You know how some assistant principals have been delegated the three B's—books, buses, and butts. Don't be guilty of that practice.

We find, too, that an additional time waster related to delegation is the inability or unwillingness to delegate. You cannot do everything yourself. Even if you know that the person to whom you're delegating a task cannot perform it as well as you can, delegate it and then help that person learn to do it better. That person will learn and you will be freed to do some of the more important tasks.

MEETINGS

One of the negatives about being a school administrator is that you will attend more than your share of meetings. Some of the meetings you will call; others, you will be asked to attend. Let's focus on the meetings you will call.

Before you call a meeting, ask yourself, "Is this meeting necessary?" Instead of calling people together, could you send a memo? Don't call meetings simply for the sake of following a routine (i.e., avoid the "It's Monday; therefore, a meeting is necessary" syndrome). If you call a meeting, have a specific purpose in mind and then decide who should attend. Who will be concerned about the topics to be discussed? Who has the information needed in the discussion? Just because it may be called a "faculty meeting" does not imply that every faculty member needs to attend. If you find that meetings are not helping you meet organizational and personal goals, then they are time wasters, and neither you nor your staff has time to waste.

LACK OF OBJECTIVES, PRIORITIES, PLANNING

To be an effective leader, you must have a vision for your organization. You must work with others to develop a vision for what you want to accomplish. This vision will then guide your actions and lead you to write goals and objectives and to plan strategies. Without vision and plans, getting sidetracked or caught up in activities unrelated to your goals is virtually assured. Dunlap notes the importance of goal setting, "The important thing is to *have* a goal, for having a goal arouses a certain inner dignity that flare-ups in your daily working environment can rarely penetrate" [69].

CRISIS MANAGEMENT

There is still the perception that, when confronted with crisis situations, women become emotional and irrational. To paraphrase lines from Rudyard Kipling's poem "If"; if you are able to keep your head when all around you are losing theirs, you won't be a man, my sister, you will be a leader [70].

One of the difficulties in dealing with crises is that you never know when they will happen or what issues will be involved. As a school administrator, you will face a range of crises (e.g., clogged toilets, teacher unrest, student violence). Whatever the situation, remain calm (at least outwardly), get as many facts as possible, know the appropriate policies and procedures, and make the best decision you can. If you discover that your decision was a bad one, just make another decision — a good one — as quickly as possible. The point is, when you face a crisis, don't be afraid to act once you have the information you need.

If you are a school administrator, you will have crises—expect them. (Be careful not to make everything a crisis, however.) When the crisis is over, analyze your actions and evaluate your performance. How you respond to crisis situations will greatly influence how you are perceived as a leader. Once you've survived a few crises, you'll realize that you can handle just about anything that comes your way.

ATTEMPTING TOO MUCH AT ONCE

During our first year as administrators, we suffered from an illness common to women administrators: the need to prove our worth and justify holding our positions. One symptom of our illness was our misperception that we could do everything, and that we could do it all in one day. There were days when our spirits may have been willing, but our flesh wasn't. Like us, you must realize that there is a limit to how much you can accomplish in a day. Then you must *stop testing your limits!*

You might be interested to learn, however, that research by Ramey, as quoted in Loden, indicates that the brains of women allow them to manage many things at once.

> While it is difficult to separate the role of society and the role of the brain in shaping behavior, it looks as if the female brain is the kind of brain that should be able to handle several problems at once with less difficulty. In fact, it has long been one of the accepted characteristics of woman that she appears, with less internal pain, to be able to shift attention quickly from one thing to another. She has a brain which can shuttle information back and forth between hemispheres—both emotional and rational information that can help her solve problems and manage many tasks. [71]

Just think of it! The female brain has almost 40 percent more connective fiber between the two hemispheres than does the male brain [72]. However just because you *can* do many things at once doesn't mean you *have* to!

CLUTTERED DESK/PERSONAL DISORGANIZATION

Don't believe the sign, "A clean desk is the sign of a cluttered mind." There is no one best way to organize. Some of us are very neat; only the materials we are using are visible on the desk. For others, our desks are in varying degrees of disarray. What you need is an organizational system that works for you. If your messy desk negatively affects your productivity, get some help. You can purchase various organizing files, boxes, drawer inserts, etc. If used conscientiously, they can bring some order to your life. Organizational methods seem idiosyncratic; my system of organization may drive you mad. Our advice is to choose a system that works for you.

The ever increasing amount of paper in our personal and professional lives has become a major problem. Computers, fax machines, and copiers are plastering our lives with paper. Take care not to become a pack rat. Keep a large trash can handy each time you open your mail, and use it! Posner recommends that you (or, better still, your secretary) separate your paperwork into four separate categories as it comes in: immediate action, pending, information, to be filed [73]. Other sorting techniques may work for you just as well. The important thing is to have a system and then to follow through with the system.

INDECISION, PROCRASTINATION

In *In Search of Excellence,* Peters and Waterman advocate abandoning the old "Get ready! Aim! Fire!" philosophy and adopting instead a new "Ready! Fire! Aim!" approach. They talk about the action orientation and how organizational success hinges on it [74]. Indecision and procrastination have many causes, including fear and laziness. Putting off making a decision (and delaying action), however, wastes valuable time. We're not implying that you should make snap judgments, but there are going to be times when you have to make decisions before you have all the data. Luckily, women seem to have a keenly developed intuitive ability that allows them ". . . to take a quantum leap and accurately judge a situation on the basis of limited conscious data" [75]. Use your intuition! Have faith in your ability to make decisions!

INABILITY TO SAY "NO"

Because women have been socialized to be accommodating and accepting, many find it difficult to say no. If you hope to be an effective administrator, the ability to say no (even if you feel guilty about doing so) is critical.

Everyone knows that if you want a job done and done well, you call on a busy person. In virtually every work setting, a few people tend to be involved in everything. They are called on whenever something extra needs to be done. To some degree, accepting additional duties is meritorious. Some of you may feel that you have gotten to this point in your administrative careers because of the extra time you spent doing tasks that others wouldn't. You've also probably learned a lot as a result of taking on those extra duties. There comes a time, though, when for your own sake, you need to say "no" – and that time is when you become a school administrator. If you don't learn to say no then, we can assure you that you will be "dumped on" over and over again.

The next time you're asked to do something, stop and ask yourself how the request fits into your personal and professional goals. Does it help you? Your school? A student? A teacher? Could someone else handle the task? Be selective with those "yes's" you hand out, and preserve time for yourself that could be put to better use.

Communicating

The community made no secret that Betty had not been their choice for the principalship of Archaic High School. The school had never been headed by a woman and, despite Betty's outstanding record of leadership as an assistant principal, the community remained convinced that a woman simply could not project the image needed to maintain the kind of discipline they wanted in their school. Now that she had been given the position, Betty knew that a major challenge she faced was convincing the parents she could handle the job. As she waited to be introduced at Archaic's first PTA meeting for the year, she prayed that the hours she had spent practicing her speech before the bedroom mirror would pay off. Determined to communicate strength and confidence, she had not only rehearsed the carefully chosen words, but her gestures, facial expressions, and intonations as well.

Dressed in her black, tailored "power suit," Betty moved to the podium. As she looked into a sea of what seemed like hostile faces, she feared that everyone would hear her palpitating heart and notice that the paper she held so tightly in her hand had gone limp from moisture. Betty's inner voice reminded her, "Take hold of yourself, Betty. Take hold."

Your ability to communicate with others is essential to your success as a school administrator. As a communicator you are both a sender and a receiver of information. Everything you say and do communicates something. The outfit you decide to wear to work says something just as clearly to the people you encounter as do the words you speak at a board meeting.

A key to successful communication is being a good listener. A good listener pays "close attention to what is being said by others and how it is being stated" [76]. To listen effectively, you must be prepared to listen. Your mind has to be receptive to the information, there can be few distractions, and you must have any necessary listening tools (e.g., pad and pencil) at hand. If people are going to communicate with you, you must make them feel comfortable. A degree of trust, an appropriate setting, and inviting nonverbal clues, such as smiles and eye contact, help to put the speaker at ease.

As you listen, be aware of your biases. Know which words or actions by the speaker result in an automatic negative response in you. Concentrate on what is being said; make eye contact with the speaker. Listen for the key elements—exactly what is the point?

Sometimes you must read between the lines. Try not to make a judgment too soon and, by all means, don't interrupt, and don't get mad. When I was an assistant principal, my principal told me, "You can't deal rationally with irrational people." As an administrator, it is important simply to listen. When an irate parent confronts you, don't try to argue or explain your position. Just listen! Frequently, that's all you need to do to diffuse the situation. Also, when you're listening you can't say anything you'll later regret!

In addition to being a good listener, you must be able to get your message across clearly and with credibility. As a woman, you communicate differently from your male counterparts. We feel that these differences are to our advantage in that they tend to accentuate our concerns for building relationships rather than establishing authority. You must remember, however, that our communication differences can be taken by others as frivolous, too tentative, or too wishy-washy. We present this section, then, not as a criticism of how women speak but as information for you as you become more aware of how your communication may affect others. According to Hunsaker and Hunsaker [77]:

- Women tend to use more adjectives than men, and those adjectives are typically more nonspecific or "fluffy" (e.g., I had a *divine* evening).
- Women tend to add a question at the end of a statement so the statement appears to be less directive (e.g., I'd like to begin the meeting at ten o'clock, *OK?*).
- Women tend to employ intonation to make their statements sound more like questions.
- Women tend to use more qualifiers (e.g., *I believe, I guess, in my opinion*).
- Women tend to overpronounce words; they focus on being ultracorrect and super polite.
- Women tend to use disclaimers more than men (e.g., *I'm not sure if I heard this right but*).
- Women tend to use more fillers, such as "um" and "uh."
- Women apologize more than men.

Remember that while these speech patterns are not negative in themselves, they may be interpreted as such. We suggest that you tape several of your conversations and presentations. Listen to yourself. Which of these behaviors do you exhibit? Do you perceive them as dysfunctional? You may then want to have a *trusted* male colleague listen to your tapes and give you feedback.

We feel that a more potent factor than what you say and how you say it is your credibility. Do people trust you? Do they believe you? Are they confident that you'll never misguide them intentionally? Hunsaker and Hunsaker list six factors that affect your credibility: expertness, motives, reliability, warmth/friendliness, dynamism (i.e., how assertive, emphatic, or forceful you are), and the opinions of others [78]. You should work every day to build your credibility quotient, for without credibility your message (no matter how substantial or powerfully delivered) carries little weight.

One of the most terrifying experiences for many of us is *the speech*. Somehow, just the thought of standing in front of a room, staring into faces you perceive as expectant, hostile, judgmental, and apathetic is enough to bring on palpitations, sweaty palms, jerky movements, and "cotton mouth." Unfortunately, we can't tell you these will go away with experience and training. Our experiences show us, however, that these reactions become less debilitating with experience; you learn to live with them, to make excellent presentations even as you "shake in your boots."

Many excellent guides have been written to help public speakers. What follows is what we find to be their best advice coupled with what we've learned through the years.

(1) Don't be a Winnie Wing-it! Prepare and practice. Certainly, there will be times when you're called to speak "off the cuff." If so, be brief and factual. On all other speaking occasions, plan, plan, plan, and practice!

(2) Organize your presentation well, using an introduction, a body, and a summary or conclusion. The old adage many of us learned about writing applies here too: "First, tell them what you're going to tell them. Then, tell them. Finally, tell them what you told them."

(3) As a part of the planning process, you must know as much as possible about your audience and what they hope to get from your presentation. Only when you know these two things can you plan appropriately.

(4) Use simple language. Don't try to impress people with big words. Try to impress them with the clarity with which you express your ideas.

(5) Be interesting. You can tell appropriate jokes or stories. You can use visuals. You can use pace, intonation, and the loudness or softness of your voice to add interest and variety to your presentation. Two words of caution are important here, however. Use techniques that are comfortable for you. For example, while both of us speak to groups frequently, neither of us feels comfortable with jokes. We, therefore, seldom use them. Secondly, when illustrating or making points with jokes, stories, and visuals, take care that they are not offensive. Nothing can destroy your credibility and your message more quickly than a joke that is inappropriate or one that hurts someone's feelings.

(6) If you're speaking in a place new to you, arrive early. Test the microphone, the overhead projector, etc. Make sure that the seating is arranged appropriately and that you can see over the podium.

(7) Speak *to* the individuals in your audience; not *at* them. We like to arrive early and mingle with some of the audience. This practice is especially helpful if you know no one. You can learn a name or two and personalize your presentation a bit. Make eye contact with members of the audience. Eye contact enhances your credibility, focuses the audience's attention, and helps you read your audience.

(8) Be sensitive to your audience. If you sense you're losing the audience, quicken the pace, skip the less interesting parts of your speech, and finish quickly.

(9) Watch your hands. Hands should be used for emphasis. Their movement should be natural. Rarely would we suggest keeping hands hidden behind the podium or your back. That stance

appears too defensive; it inhibits your communication. In normal conversation, we use our hands constantly. Think of a speech as a conversation and use your hands accordingly. Posner advises that you never let your hands drop below your waist [79]. Hands should facilitate the communication. Watch a video of yourself and notice your hands. Were they distracting? Or, did they help you make important points?

(10) Be enthusiastic. If you're not excited about what you're saying, no one else will be either. Let the audience know where you stand. You convey your enthusiasm through smiles, facial expressions and gestures, your posture, your impeccable grooming, and your sensitivity to the audience. (A tip here: always end your speech a few minutes early rather than a few minutes late.)

FACILITATING CHANGE

A leader is typically defined as a person who has the ability to help people want to change. She is the person who has a vision, who has the ability to help others develop a vision, and who is willing to take the risks necessary to make the vision a reality. Helping people change is dependent upon your ability to understand where they're coming from. Developing a vision means talking to people, it means sharing, and it starts with the development of a group vision. We've been around long enough to know that taking this initiative is not easy. We also know that it's improbable that you will have 100 percent support. Some will openly oppose you and your ideas, others will surreptitiously try to undermine you, and others will simply "go along for the ride," taking the path of least resistance. But you still have to work to sell, sell, sell; persuade, persuade, persuade; trade, trade, trade.

A change agent (i.e., a leader) must take risks. Posner defines taking a risk as "betting on yourself" and "betting on chance" (the probability that things will go in your favor). He points out that risk taking may also be betting on others, since when you bet on others you're betting on your judgment of their abilities [80]. Let's face it, women administrators are risk-takers. They've had to take risks to get where they are. Each of them has had to ask herself just how far she was willing to go to achieve her objective. Many of them have taken giant leaps; others have taken baby steps. Either way, they've probably grown and made their next risk-taking venture easier. Posner [81] offers the following advice to risk-takers:

- Make sure that the risks are justified.
- Don't discount intuition.
- Confront the fears that may be holding you back – fear of failure, uncertainty, disapproval.
- Know your limitations.
- Always have a clear idea of how much authority you have and how much power you wield.
- Have a contingency plan.
- Gauge in advance just how far you can go.
- Go for maximum impact.
- Know when to quit.

Dealing with Subordinates

At the end of my first year as principal, a teacher with thirty-five years of teaching experience admitted that because she had never worked for a "lady principal," she was quite concerned when she heard I had been assigned to the school. Assuming that I would be "cliquish and moody like women tend to be," she had decided to retire. Fortunately for the school (she was an incredibly skilled teacher), several of her colleagues convinced her to delay her retirement for at least a semester. During that time she observed me closely, she said, paying particular attention to where I sat during lunch and in other social situations, to whom I talked, and whether or not I seemed to show favoritism. When I asked if she had scrutinized the actions of the former male principal so closely, she shrugged and responded, "But you know how women are."

One reality women administrators must confront is that when a man enters the principal's office, he begins with an advantage. The expectation is that he will succeed. Women do not enjoy such an advantage. The expectation for them is failure. Unlike their male counterparts, the actions of women administrators are closely scrutinized by teachers looking for evidence of behaviors to confirm their expectations of failure. Should teachers fail to find such evidence and be forced to acknowledge the woman's leadership ability, the negative stereotype about women leaders is only dented—not destroyed. Only *that* woman is accepted. In fact, her performance is likely to be viewed as atypical and therefore not applicable to other women. So the next woman administrator (if a woman does, in fact, succeed her) must prove herself all over again.

The reactions of women teachers to women administrators run the gamut. While some women teachers applaud the fact that a female has achieved a position of leadership in a male-dominated world, and often regard her as a role model (a cross that the female administrator may find difficult to bear), other women teachers may be troubled by what they view as a disruption in the social order. Many teachers still view the principalship as a male domain and may resist leadership from another female. This resistance is particularly evident if the woman administrator employs an autocratic leadership style. Still other women teachers may view the accomplishments of a female administrator as a kind of personal affront. These women may have grown accustomed to using their gender as an excuse for not seeking an administrative position (their actions reflect the "Because I'm a woman I won't get the job anyway so why even apply" attitude). With the presence of the female administrator, the validity of their argument is called into question.

For female administrators, perhaps more threatening than dealing with female teachers is the prospect of dealing with male teachers. Like female teachers, the reactions of male teachers also run the gamut. First, let us acknowledge that many male teachers accept leadership without regard to the gender of the leader. Such men simply do their jobs and do their best to help the principal do his or hers. The astute administrator—male or female—never takes such people for granted, and acknowledges their efforts.

On the other hand, there are male teachers who are threatened by women administrators. Most men have been socialized to lead women — not to be led by them. Faced with this paradox, many men do not know quite how to respond. If the female administrator has a male assistant, some male teachers may try to circumvent the female by dealing directly with the assistant. Our advice is to stop such action immediately by communicating honestly and openly with the teacher and the assistant principal.

Other male teachers may try to demean the role the female administrator plays. The message these men communicate is: "I'll play along as long as you don't seriously think I regard you as the boss. In other words, just let me have my way and I'll humor you." When confrontations arise with such teachers (and they will), the female administrator must clearly establish herself as "boss."

Another strategy used by male teachers is to try to charm the female administrator. That is, men engage in behaviors they think are supposed to flatter females. For example, instead of complimenting the female administrator on the substance of her speech, they concentrate on how stunning she looks delivering it. After I had spoken at a PTA meeting one night, a male faculty member shook my hand and remarked, "That is some outfit you're wearing. It must have set your husband back at least a couple hundred bucks." My response was quick and direct, "And what do you think about the goals I presented?" When he was unable to respond intelligently, he learned that I valued his ability to listen far more than his ability to look.

Because each situation is unique, the best we can offer are general guidelines. We urge female administrators to keep in mind that attitudes die hard. If you focus on doing your job well, being fair and consistent in your dealings with your staff, and respecting the dignity of each person with whom you interact, you may see a metamorphosis right before your very eyes.

Advice for Black Women

We were tempted not to include this section, because black women and white women share many of the same problems as they attempt to survive in the male-dominated world of school administration. But we believe that, in many cases, black women must take extra measures to be successful.

Although Doughty refers to the collective group of black administrators as "invisible" [82], we doubt that this will be your individual experience. In fact, if for no other reason than the fact that you are "different," you will stand out. Getting lost in the crowd or blending into the background may not be options available to you. Many of your colleagues will quickly find out everything they can about your personal and professional life. Rather than trying to avoid the spotlight, learn to bask in it with grace and poise.

If you are the only woman or the only black administrator in your school district, be prepared to juggle more responsibilities than your male colleagues. Expect to be asked to serve on far more committees than you can possibly handle, but be selective about the committees you choose and the meetings you attend. Do not deceive yourself into thinking that you are necessarily invited to meetings for your ideas. Sometimes, all that is wanted is your presence. Nothing more.

You are both black and female; expect to have your competence and skills questioned. Don't become defensive or angry when it happens. Just view it as part of your rite of passage. Provided you stick to your standards with rigor and determination, the respect you deserve will come in time.

You may experience internal and external conflict. Resolve it as best you can. If you were selected for the job over a black male, you can expect criticism from those who feel you are contributing to the problems faced by black men. You may also be resented by other females who would prefer to maintain the status quo. You've got to sort out your feelings and attempt to resolve whatever conflict might be present.

Many of your colleagues and staff members will expect you to see racism and sexism in virtually everything. Disappoint them. When problems arise, resist the temptation to make them race- or gender-related until you have explored and eliminated other possibilities. If you tend to make most situations race- or gender-related, you will become ineffective and stereotyped. Save charges of racism and sexism for situations that clearly warrant them, but do not fail to speak out when such situations occur!

Finally, you will have the opportunity to help other women and minorities. Do so enthusiastically. Clearing the hurdles and becoming a school administrator should be far more than a personal accomplishment; we hope it will also represent an opportunity for you to help others gain entry into the system.

Conclusion

This chapter has focused on a variety of skills and traits essential to effective leadership. We've paid particular attention to building interpersonal relationships, managing time, communicating, and facilitating change. Our discussion of these skills has been isolated, with emphasis placed on each out of context of the hurly-burly of real life. The printed text makes such treatment necessary although we know that in our day-to-day existence, interpersonal relations impact communications, which impact change, and so forth. We know, too, that our lives on the job affect our personal lives and vice versa. The final chapter concentrates on what we call the "self" dimension of leadership.

5

Balancing Your Life

After I left the principalship, a friend asked why I had chosen to leave when everything seemed to be going so well. Student achievement and staff morale were at an all-time high, and parents were ecstatic. After considerable time for reflection, my response was simple, "I needed to regain control of my life." And that was so true. Determined to prove my qualifications and abilities not only to others but to myself as well, I had allowed the principalship to consume me. My identity—and even my self-worth to some degree—had become tied to my success as a principal. To put it simply, my life was out of balance!

Women administrators are highly susceptible to losing their sense of balance. Because most have had to struggle to attain administrative positions, they are likely to become obsessed with their jobs. In fact, many women administrators (particularly those who are single) allow their jobs to become their lives. If you are concerned about being able to balance your professional and personal lives, this chapter will offer you tips on how to keep your job in perspective and take care of your "self" dimension.

Two of the topics, "Keeping Current" and "Presenting a Professional Image," focus on taking care of yourself in your professional life. The other two topics, "Managing Stress" and "Balancing Your Life," focus on your personal life. To be a successful school administrator, we believe there must be a balance between your professional life and your personal life.

Keeping Current

In this age of information, you are inundated with things to know. While you cannot know the details of everything, it's important to be generally knowledgeable about the major issues in education, politics, and health. Our advice to you is to read, read, read. Especially important sources are local and regional newspapers, professional journals and magazines, and books. Although time-consuming, reading provides knowledge, peace, quiet, and relaxation.

If you can't find time to read, then listen. Tapes of books and even journal articles can now be purchased. If you drive frequently (or better yet, if you exercise regularly), you can use these tapes to make those minutes and hours behind the wheel of a car or an exercise bicycle intellectually productive.

It's also important to attend professional meetings and conferences. At these gatherings, you will be able to meet new people, renew acquaintances, pick up fresh ideas, and learn more about major trends and concerns within your profession. This networking may be essential to your success as a leader. One tip we'd like to share with you concerns the effective use of conference breaks. Instead of spending most of the break time standing in bathroom lines (there are never enough stalls in women's rest rooms), we suggest that you take bathroom breaks during presentations and use breaks for meeting people and building relationships. We would rather miss a few minutes of a presentation than miss the opportunity that breaks provide for networking.

Presenting a Professional Image

Each of us has an image; it is the overall perception that others have of us. Our image is created by factors such as our appearance, our speech, our demeanor, our position, and our actions. Not only do individuals have images, but we also hold expectations for certain roles. We expect our President and First Lady to have a stately, dignified demeanor. We expect ministers to look conservative, to have a composed, comforting appearance. We likewise hold certain images for principals. They are expected to exude confidence, to be articulate, to at least appear to be in charge. If you have been successful in attaining an administrative position, you have obviously projected such an image. Your challenge, however, is to maintain that image day after day. How is this feat accomplished? Let's discuss some factors you should consider.

While image involves far more than clothing, what you wear gives others an impression of who you are and what you represent. According to Thourlby [83], the minute you step into a room (even when you're known by no one there), at least ten decisions are made based solely on how you look:

(1) Economic level
(2) Educational level
(3) Trustworthiness
(4) Social position
(5) Level of sophistication
(6) Economic heritage
(7) Social heritage
(8) Educational heritage
(9) Success
(10) Moral character

While we know that our clothing and appearance reveal little about our true substance, they create a powerful first impression. They speak loudly about our credibility and our skills, despite the fact that the message may be an inaccurate one.

As a new principal, I was unaware of the messages communicated by my choice of clothing. At thirty-three, I still had a relatively youthful appearance, which I attempted to enhance by my choice of attire. Three weeks after the school year had begun, a veteran teacher who had been highly supportive of my appointment as principal called me aside and explained, "Your dresses are cute, but they don't make you look like a principal. You want people to know you're in charge." Shortly after our conversation, I invested in a few tailored suits with coordinated accessories. I can never be sure that the change in clothes made the difference, but I do know that teachers noticed and complimented me on my "new, professional look." Whether it was the clothes or the reaction of teachers to the clothes, I began to feel more in charge.

In my second year, the same veteran teacher called me aside once again. This time, however, she explained that because the staff had come to respect me as an effective leader, what I chose to wear was no longer an issue. In other words, my actions had earned me the right to wear whatever I liked. While it is unfair that women are subjected to such games, the reality is that if you are unable or unwilling to project the "right" image, you may not have the opportunity to gain the credibility you need in order to redefine that "right" image. During my second year as principal, my approach to choice of clothing was eclectic. I still wore my tailored suits when I felt the need to be perceived as "official," but I also resumed wearing my youthful dresses, blouses, and skirts. By doing so, I wanted to create a new image of what the person in the principal's office might look like. As a first-year principal, it was important to me that I earn the respect of my staff and community. Wearing suits was just one strategy I used. Once the respect had been earned, I could be myself and get on with important issues.

Managing Stress

Being a school administrator can be stressful, particularly for women who, in addition to dealing with the common stresses associated with school administration, must also contend with stresses resulting from discrimination, unwanted sexual advances, and obligations of both career and family. Even during periods of relative calm, administrators often find it difficult to relax because of the anticipation of crisis.

It is perhaps no accident of nature that women are physiologically better able to cope with stress. Loden quotes Estelle Ramey of the Georgetown Medical School in saying that the hormonal makeup of women ". . . makes them less likely to suffer from stress-related illness . . . and less apt to display aggressive behavior when placed in threatening situations" [84]. Recalling this biological advantage over your male counterparts should be reassuring to you when you are faced with the normal stresses of being a professional woman in a man's world.

To reduce stress, you need a relief system of loving, supportive people in your life—people who care for you as a person, who allow you to just be you. Also, you need a sense of humor, a willingness to laugh at yourself. Remember not to take things (including yourself) too seriously; not everything is a "do-or-die" situation. We also believe that to reduce stress, you must regularly take part in recreations you enjoy, activities that allow you to leave work physically, mentally, and emotionally. Both of us handle our stress by exercising regularly, shopping, reading, and traveling frequently. One of us even likes to fish.

Balancing Your Life: For Married Women

By the time the teachers arrive at 7:45 A.M., Mary has been at work at least forty-five minutes. Each day she arrives at 7:00 to greet children dropped off by parents on their way to work. She could have assigned this job to her teachers, but she is determined to relieve them of as many non-instructional duties as possible. Besides, she thought that getting to school early every day would give her a head start on her work. She was wrong. With almost fifty early-arriving youngsters, Mary has found little time for anything except supervising them.

When the school day begins at 8:00, she moves from one task to another. Although she tries to plan her days, she never knows what problems might arise. One of the things she's learned about being a school administrator is the importance of being flexible. By lunch, she has held two parent conferences, ordered textbooks for a teacher, administered first aid to three children with nose bleeds, conducted a classroom observation, written six memos, met with the school custodian, returned six phone calls, and disciplined four students.

When the teachers leave at 3:00 P.M., Mary returns to her office where she finishes reading her mail, returns phone calls, and tries to catch her breath. When she finally checks her watch, she is shocked to discover that it is already 5:00 P.M. Although she'd like to go home to check on her husband and children, she wonders if it's worth the twenty-minute drive since there's a PTA meeting scheduled for 7:00. She decides to go home anyway. When she arrives, she finds a letter from her son's school requesting a parent conference. Much to her surprise, her son is failing math. As she pops the frozen dinners into the microwave for the third time this week, she senses her husband's frustration. She can only wonder if anyone senses hers.

If you're the typical female candidate who is anxious to become an administrator, our advice is to carefully consider the time constraints and pressures: don't take on the challenge of an administrative position unless you're a skilled juggler. Despite the responsibilities of your career, you may find that the care of the home will still be regarded primarily as your domain. While your husband may assist, he is likely to regard his actions as "helping you out." You can certainly attempt to change his perception, but realize that change will take time.

DEFINING YOUR ROLES

If you're going to balance your roles and responsibilities successfully, you will first have to determine what they are. Exactly what is expected of you? Begin by examining the different roles you currently play. Stop for a moment and make a list. Include on your list all the roles you are expected to assume. No doubt your list will be quite long and may include roles such as: mother, wife, daughter, or community leader. Go ahead and list them all, using Figure 5.

Once you have listed the roles, the next step is to prioritize the different roles. Which ones are really important and which ones are

Roles I Am Expected to Assume
1.
2.
3.
4.
5.
6.
7.
8.
9.

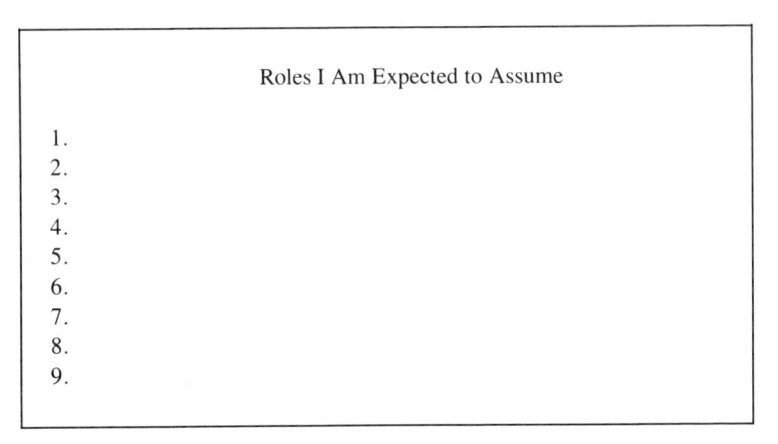

Figure 5. Identifying your roles.

not so critical? The purpose for doing this exercise is to decide where you will devote your time and energy *at this point in your life*. The purpose is *not* to determine necessarily which role is most important to you. For example, during my first year as principal, I decided that the role to which I would devote my time and energy was the principalship. I therefore suspended my doctoral studies, resigned from several leadership positions in the church and community, and reallocated household responsibilities to my husband and children. Did my decision to devote my time and energy to the principalship indicate that I valued this role more than being a student, community leader, wife, or mother? Of course not. My actions merely indicated that I was wise enough to realize that I couldn't be all things to all people. Like most mortals, I have but so much energy, and rather than diffuse it I wanted to focus my efforts. There was no pressing timetable for the completion of my doctorate, there were others in the church and community who could provide leadership, and, given the fact that our children were old enough to be somewhat independent (eight and eleven years old), I felt comfortable with my decision to focus my energies on the principalship. Had I been writing my dissertation, or had my children been preschool age, my decision might have been different.

If you are aspiring to an administrative position, analyze your situation, think through your options carefully, discuss those options and their implications with those affected, and then make a decision. Once the decision is made, fight off feelings of guilt or regret. If feelings of guilt or regret persist, our advice to you is make another decision that provides the psychological comfort you need.

Now that you won't feel guilty about the order in which you prioritize your roles for this (or next) year, go ahead and list them. We have purposely provided space in Figure 6 for three roles. We hope you won't feel compelled to add other roles. Remember that the fewer roles you choose, the more concentrated your efforts can be.

Now that you've defined the roles on which you will concentrate, the next step is to define what responsibilities each role entails. In other words, what specific responsibilities do you have as a mother? Are you expected to prepare daily meals for your family, clean the house regularly, carpool the children, assist children with homework, plan social outings, etc.? What are your responsibilities as president of a local sorority? Although we realize that your list will not be all-inclusive, be sure to include all major responsibilities (see Figure 7).

Now that you have listed the responsibilities for each of the roles, let's look at them and decide if any changes are necessary. Can you still be a good mother and not cook three meals a day? We certainly hope so. Must cleaning be a part of your daily routine? Strike any responsibilities that you feel are unnecessary or unimportant. Having done that, you are now left with responsibilities that

---

The Roles to Which I Will Devote
My Time and Energy This (or Next) Year (in Priority Order)

1.
2.
3.

Figure 6. Prioritizing your roles.

> Responsibilities of Roles
> to Which I Will Devote My Time and Energy This (or Next) Year
>
> Role:
> Responsibilities:
>
>
>
> Role:
> Responsibilities:
>
>
>
> Role:
> Responsibilities:

Figure 7. Identifying role responsibilities.

you feel are both necessary and important. The next question is, are you the only or the best person to carry out each responsibility? Are there other family members or persons to whom one or more responsibilities might be assigned? The earlier you insist that household tasks be shared by family members, the earlier you are on your way to balancing your life and maintaining some degree of sanity. If you feel that the responsibilities are important but are unwilling or unable to share them with other family members, then a viable option might be to explore the possibility of obtaining professional domestic help.

Women administrators tend to be highly motivated and to have records of outstanding achievement. Because they are used to being the best at what they do, many have trouble settling for anything less than perfection. One of the first steps in balancing your life is to be willing not only to reduce the number of roles you play, but also to adjust your standards in some of those roles. You cannot excel in everything you do. That doesn't mean that you're any less competent; it only means you're human. You're kidding yourself if you think you can be rated "ten" as a wife, mother, principal, and community leader. The earlier you accept that fact, the earlier others will, too.

DEALING WITH SPOUSES

As we have listened to women discuss their fears about becoming school administrators, one of the fears most often cited by married women is the impact that the job might have on their relationships with their husbands. Since each marital relationship is unique, we would not presume to make any generalizations. We will instead pose a few questions for the consideration of married women who may be contemplating becoming school administrators.

(1) Have you and your husband (or significant other) discussed the specific responsibilities that the administrative position you are seeking entails?

(2) Have you been open and honest about sensitive issues that might be of concern to your husband (e.g., the fact that you will be interacting regularly with men in social settings, that your schedule will be hectic, and that there may be times when he will not know where you are, etc.)?

(3) Assuming you and your husband have communicated openly and honestly, how does he feel about your becoming an administrator? Is he supportive, neutral, or nonsupportive? The best situation, of course, is to have a supportive husband; the worst is for him to be nonsupportive. A female administrator whose husband is nonsupportive is unquestionably swimming against the tide. Not only is it likely that she will struggle with his lack of support for her role in the workplace, but it is also likely that she will face a lack of support in her role at home. Women with unsupportive spouses express feelings of isolation, alienation, resentment, and even hostility.

Should your husband be unsupportive of your plan to become a school administrator, it might be helpful to attempt to determine his reasons. Like most men, it's likely that he's been socialized to be your protector; his concerns might therefore be based primarily upon his desire to protect you from what he perceives to be the hardships of leadership. Chances are that if you've known each other for any period of time, however, he realizes that you are a risk-taker. If he doesn't, try to help him understand that whether you succeed or not, you deserve the opportunity to attempt the challenge.

There are men who may feel threatened or insecure about the prospect of their wives becoming a "boss." Whether such reactions are as common as women indicate, the fear of this reaction is indeed real for many women. One of the problems in dealing with husbands who may feel threatened or insecure is that they often deny such feelings. Their actions (subtle though they may be), however, indicate pent-up hostility and anger. Retaliation through verbal attacks on their wives regarding their inadequacy as mothers or wives is not uncommon.

During a conversation with Janet, one of our students who recently became a high school assistant principal, she explained that her ten-year-old son's teacher had called to inform her of her son's misbehavior in class. She then reminded herself, "My husband said this would happen if I moved into administration. He warned me that I couldn't be a good mother if I took this job." Continued discussion revealed that despite the changes in her professional life, Janet and her husband had made no adjustments in their personal lives. She was still expected to fulfill the traditional duties of wife and mother (e.g., cleaning, cooking, and child rearing) while he continued to focus on his career.

In response to Janet's dilemma, I shared a personal anecdote. During my tenure as principal, I arrived at home one evening and found my husband, who was also a principal, lying down resting. Although we both had come home to a dirty house and two hungry children, I was the only one who seemed bothered. Sensing my frustration, my husband inquired, "What do you need?" With no hesitation whatsoever, I responded, "A wife." His response, which was as spontaneous as mine had been, shocked me. "So do I," he said. The next day we hired a housekeeper.

Women who enter administration with the expectation that they can continue to fulfill their traditional roles are setting themselves up for disappointment, frustration, and guilt. Couples need to recognize that role changes for the wife most assuredly will necessitate role changes for the husband, particularly if young children are involved.

As part of the Women's Institute, a group of veteran women principals and superintendents were invited to share their experiences with aspiring and newly appointed women school administrators. During the discussion, the veteran administrators were asked to identify what they considered to be the most important quality a prospective school administrator should look for in a husband. The consensus of the veteran administrators was, "Someone who is secure." In a private conversation after the presentation, one of the veteran principals who had been recently divorced elaborated on the importance of having a secure spouse. She explained that her ex-husband often complained of being regarded as her "appendage." Her role as principal had made her highly visible in the community. Her husband had neither the status nor the recognition afforded her and was often known as "Mrs. Anderson's husband." His strong resentment was finally verbalized during an argument when he exclaimed, "The trouble here is we've got our places mixed up. You belong to me—I don't belong to you!" They are divorced and neither "belongs" to either now.

DEALING WITH CHILDREN

If you are a woman administrator with children, you may also have to deal with your children's feelings about your role. Your children's reactions, however, will usually depend upon the extent to which you have already been involved in leadership activities. Most women administrators have held a variety of leadership roles in their communities. If you're atypical in that regard, and your children have been used to having you all to themselves, then you will need to give them a crash course in being independent. The ages of your children will, of course, be a critical factor. Be assured, however, that assuming the role of school administrator does not mean that you will not respond to your children's needs. Rather, it means that you will expect your children to gain some degree of independence and to be selective about making demands on your time. If your children are old enough to assume household responsibilities, then insist that they do so. Remember, you are not only teaching them responsibility, you are also reinforcing the fact that families share responsibilities and work together.

Another extremely important lesson that you are teaching your children concerns the roles of men and women. By seeing you in action, your sons learn that women can be in charge. Your daughters learn that in addition to being mothers and wives, they can be leaders as well. It is these messages that will hopefully be passed down through the generations and ultimately bring about changes in how children are socialized.

Balancing your life dictates that you communicate with those affected by your decisions. While the final decision about whether or not to seek an administrative position will rest with you, we urge you to make that decision only after carefully considering the implications for those who might be affected by it. We wish we could provide you with a checklist that would enable you to make the best decision, but you're smart enough to know that each woman will have to develop her own checklist reflecting her own situation and values. Our best advice is to try to involve your family and others whose personal lives might be affected by your decision in open, honest communication. Think about what you want and what they want. Weigh the pros and cons. Make a decision and then don't look back. Both guilt and regret are worthless emotions.

Balancing Your Life: For Single Women

Thirty-five and single, Nancy is a new principal. During the first few weeks of the school year, several older female teachers commented on her marital status. One asked, "Why isn't a pretty girl like you married?" Another cautioned her about getting too old to have children. Still another hinted that she'd like to "fix her up" with her bachelor son.

Nancy has also had to deal with the sexual innuendos of a married fellow principal who has suggested that thirtysomething single women are either "loose" or "frigid." He's offered to give her a personal "test" to find out which term best describes her. So far Nancy has decided to ignore his advances but fears that she will soon have to deal with him more aggressively.

Yesterday Nancy began to think about the upcoming faculty social. She'd like to invite an old friend as her escort but knows that if she does, certain faculty will question her about him, and she just doesn't feel like dealing with their questions. Others will assume that wedding plans are in the making. A few will wonder if she can do a good job as principal if she gets too involved with someone. So Nancy contemplates going alone. That decision, however, is also fraught with problems. There will be questions and concerns, "Is she on the make?" "Why can't she get a boyfriend?" "Is she after someone's husband?" Nancy wonders if it wouldn't be easier just to stay home.

We realize that many of you are not married. As we mentioned in the Preface, this is also the case for one of us. One of the biggest problems with being a single (either divorced, never married, or widowed) school administrator is the fact that others will expect you to have unlimited free time to devote to work. Beware of falling into that trap. We encourage you to prioritize your roles as explained in the section "Balancing Your Life: For Married Women" and organize your time toward the fulfillment of these roles. Once you've done that, you can get on with living a balanced life.

To be sure, married and single women administrators share many of the same problems. However, as a single woman, you may face situations in the workplace that your married women colleagues are less likely to encounter. Following is a brief discussion of three of those problems.

DEALING WITH MARRIED MEN

As a school administrator, you will not only be moving into a man's world, but into a married man's world, as well. For many men, working with you as an equal will be a novel experience. Furthermore, working with you as a single woman may present them with a different set of challenges.

There are two categories of men whom I have found to be problematic in the workplace:

(1) There are those who are so uncomfortable with my presence that they tend to avoid me or are overly cautious in their dealings with me.
(2) There are those who are so comfortable with my presence that they take unearned liberties.

How you deal with each of these types of men differs significantly.

With the former type of men (those who may be uncomfortable with your presence), my advice is to be open and approachable but always professional. Nudge or gently push yourself into their world. Volunteer to serve on committees with them and then chair the committee. Seize opportunities to interact with them; however, let there be no doubt that you are only interested in a professional relationship. Nothing more. For more reasons than I can enumerate, many of these men will feel threatened by your presence and will never accept you as their equal. My advice is not to expend too much time or energy trying to convince them of your skills. Just make sure they have opportunities to see you as the professional that you are. You can do nothing more. The rest is up to them.

I find the second category of men more offensive but easier to handle. Married men who are overly comfortable with your presence and who may be tempted to take unearned liberties need to be dealt with in a direct, straightforward manner. At the first sign of trouble, speak up and clearly explain the boundaries of your relationship. Meanwhile, you should find out the school district's procedures for dealing with sexual harassment and make it clear to the potential offender that – should it be necessary – you will report his actions to the proper authorities. Should the harassment continue, follow through!

DEALING WITH SPOUSES OF MARRIED MEN

In addition to being viewed with suspicion by married male colleagues, the wives of your colleagues may also present a challenge. They may fear the relationship between you and their spouse and regard you as a threat to their marriage. My advice is to be friendly with your colleagues' wives and refrain from doing anything that might give them reason to question your relationship with their husbands.

An attractive woman administrator who was recently divorced and whose husband was also an administrator indicated that while they were married, she had no problem being accepted by other administrators and their spouses. Since being divorced, however, she commented that both the administrators and their wives tended to shun her in social situations. To address this problem, she makes an effort to find a male escort to accompany her to social gatherings. Only when she is escorted do the administrators and their wives seem comfortable interacting with her.

DEALING WITH SINGLE MEN IN THE OFFICE AND SOCIALLY

Dealing with single men, especially those whom you might want to date, can also be a challenge for women administrators. Many will see you as a "boss" and be intimidated. Your challenge is to get them to realize that you can be a boss and still be warm, friendly, and vulnerable. If, despite your efforts, a man is so intimidated by your professional position that he cannot see your personal side, then think seriously about whether or not you want to pursue a serious relationship with him.

We hope your warmth and understanding show through your professional "in charge" exterior. It is difficult, however, to move from "Ms. in Charge" to "Ms. Please Make All the Decisions for Me." There are several ways to handle this situation.

(1) You can decide to have only "fun" relationships where you date several different men and pass up (at least for the time being) a long-term, intimate relationship.
(2) You may find a perfect partner, one who is willing to be your equal in a give-and-take relationship.
(3) You may decide that the most important role you play right now is that of school administrator, and thereby sublimate the role of "hot date" or "intimate partner."

We think any of these roles may be appropriate. You have to decide. But we want to caution you about one type of relationship: be careful about becoming involved in a traditional relationship where the male is the dominant partner who makes all the decisions, who expects dinner (and no Lean Cuisines either) on the table every night at 5:00, and who demands that you account for all your time away from home.

We believe that the important thing is to be happy and productive, to find time for yourself and those you love while building your career. How you do it is a personal and sometimes difficult decision.

We doubt that your life will be perfect after reading this book. We do hope, however, that we've helped you to put things in perspective. You are far more than the sum of your parts. How each part interacts with the other parts will substantially impact the quality of your life. We encourage you to be a reflective, caring woman who knows how to balance her personal needs with the demands of the job, home, and society. We wish you success and happiness.

Appendix

In addition to the sources provided in the Bibliography, we recommend the following books:

Bixler, S. 1984. *The Professional Image*. New York, NY: The Putnam Publishing Group.

Bixler, S. 1991. *Professional Presence*. New York, NY: G. P. Putnam's Sons.

Culp, S. 1990. *Conquering the Paper Pile-Up*. Cincinnati, OH: Writer's Digest Books.

Helgesen, S. 1990. *The Female Advantage: Women's Ways of Leadership*. New York, NY: Doubleday.

Naisbitt, J. and P. Aburden. 1990. *Megatrends 2000: Ten New Directions for the 1990's*. New York, NY: William Morrow and Co., Inc.

Pearce, C. A. 1990. *Career Chic: What Every Woman Should Know about Getting Ahead in Style*. New York, NY: The Putnam Publishing Group.

Wilder, C. 1990. *The Presentations Kit: Ten Steps for Selling Your Ideas*. New York, NY: John Wiley and Sons, Inc.

Courses for women in school administration are offered at:

Eastern Michigan University
Continuing Education
Ypsilanti, MI 48197

Hofstra University
Department of Administration and Policy Studies
Hempstead, NY 11550

University of South Carolina
Department of Educational Leadership and Policies
Columbia, SC 29208

Workshops and seminars for women in school administration are offered by:

University of Nebraska-Lincoln
Department of Educational Administration
Lincoln, NE 68588

American Association for School Administrators
1801 North Moore Street
Arlington, VA 22209

Videos:

Shortchanging Girls, Shortchanging America. 1991. American Association of University Women.

All the Wrong Moves: Sexual Harassment in the Workplace. 1987. Kinetic Films.

Sexual Harassment: It's No Game. 1987. Center for Women in Government.

Bibliography

1. Loomis, L. J. and P. Wild. 1978. "Increasing the Role of Women in Community College Administration," ERIC Document Reproduction Service No. BO ED 181 943, pp. 1–12.
2. Young, E. F. 1989. "The Highest Salaried Woman in the World," in *Women in Educational Administration*, C. Shakeshaft, ed., Newbury Park, CA: SAGE Publications, p. 18.
3. Shakeshaft, C., ed. 1989. *Women in Educational Administration*. Newbury Park, CA: SAGE Publications, p. 20.
4. National Education Association. 1990. *Rankings of the States: 1990.* Washington, DC: National Education Association, p. 17.
5. Jones, E. H. and X. P. Montenegro. 1990. *Women and Minorities in School Administration: Facts and Figures, 1989–1990.* Arlington, VA: Office of Minority Affairs, American Association of School Administrators, p. 8.
6. Jones, E. H. and X. P. Montenegro. 1985. *Women and Minorities in School Administration: Facts and Figures, 1984–85.* Arlington, VA: Office of Minority Affairs, American Association of School Administrators, p. 19.
7. Shakeshaft, C., ed., p. 20.
8. Yeakey, C. C., G. S. Johnson and J. A. Adkison. 1986. "In Pursuit of Equity: A Review of Research on Minorities and Women in Educational Administration," *Educational Administration Quarterly*, 22(3):110–149.
9. Shakeshaft, C., ed., p. 21.
10. Shakeshaft, C., ed., pp. 57–61.
11. Doughty, R. 1980. "The Black Female Administrator: Woman in a Double Bind," in *Women and Educational Leadership*, S. K. Biklen and M. B. Brannigan, eds., Lexington, MA: Lexington Books, pp. 165–174.

12. Doughty, R., p. 167.
13. Shakeshaft, C., ed., pp. 59–63.
14. Doughty, R., p. 167.
15. Adkison, J. 1981. "Women in School Administration: A Review of the Research," *Review of Educational Research*, 51(3):311–343.
16. Shakeshaft, C., ed., pp. 61–63.
17. Shakeshaft, C., ed., p. 63.
18. Shakeshaft, C., ed., pp. 40–41.
19. Shakeshaft, C., ed., pp. 46–47.
20. Young, E. F., p. 18.
21. Chancellor, W. E. 1915. *Our Schools, Their Administration and Supervision*. Boston, MA: D. C. Heath and Co., p. 183.
22. Smith, J. 1978. "Encouraging Women to Enter Administration," *NASSP Bulletin*, 62(418):114–119.
23. Owens, E. 1976. "Perceived Barriers to Employment for Women as Educational Administrators in South Carolina Public Schools," *Dissertation Abstracts International*, 36(11A):7107A.
24. Hoyle, J. 1969. "Who Shall Be Principal–A Man or a Woman?" *National Elementary Principal*, 48(3):23–24.
25. Swiderski, W. 1988. "Problems Faced by Women in Gaining Access to Administrative Positions in Education," *Education Canada*, 28(3):25–31.
26. Shakeshaft, C., ed., p. 43.
27. Shakeshaft, C., ed., p. 38.
28. National Education Association. 1905. *Report of the Committee on Salaries, Tenure, and Pensions of Public School Teachers in the United States to the National Council of Education*. Winona, MN: National Education Association, p. 19.
29. Marshall, C. 1984. "Men and Women in Educational Administration Programs," *Journal of the National Association for Women Deans, Administrators, and Counselors*, 48(1):3-12.
30. Steinem, G. 1971. "A New Egalitarian Life Style," *New York Times* (August 26):37.
31. Tannen, D. 1990. *You Just Don't Understand: Women and Men in Conversation*. New York, NY: Ballantine Books, p. 43.
32. Turbak, G. 1990. "Girls Will Be Girls," *Kiwanis Magazine*, pp. 37–40.
33. Tannen, D., p. 43.
34. Turbak, G., pp. 37–40.
35. Loomis, L. J. and P. Wild, pp. 1–12.

36. Turbak, G., pp. 37–40.
37. Good, T., J. Sikes and J. Brophy. 1973. "Effects of Teacher Sex and Student Sex in Classroom Interaction," *Journal of Educational Psychology*, 65(1):74–87.
38. Schultz, B. 1982. "Argumentativeness: Its Effect in Group Decision-Making and Its Role in Leadership Perception," *Communication Quarterly*, 30(4):368–375.
39. Clement, J. 1980. "Sex Bias in School Administration," in *Women and Educational Leadership*, S. K. Biklen and M. B. Brannigan, eds., Lexington, MA: Lexington Books, pp. 131–138.
40. Owen, W. F. 1988. "Rhetorical Themes of Emergent Female Leaders," in "Gender and Leadership: The Implications of Small Group Research," L. L. Gale, ed., *Initiatives*, 15(4):19–28.
41. McQuigg, B. D. and P. W. Carlton. 1980. "Women Administrators and America's Schools: A National Dilemma," *The High School Journal*, 64(2):50–54.
42. Ortiz, F. I. 1981. *Career Patterns in Education. Men, Women, and Minorities in Public School Administration*. New York, NY: J. F. Praeger, p. 58.
43. Fansher, T. A. and T. H. Buxton. 1984. "A Job Satisfaction Profile of the Secondary School Principal in the U.S.," *NASSP Bulletin*, 68(468):32–39.
44. Jones, E. H. and X. P. Montenegro, 1990, p. 8.
45. Shakeshaft, C., ed., p. 91.
46. Jenkins, W. J. 1966. "A Study of the Attitudes of Elementary School Teachers in Selected Schools in Montgomery County, Pennsylvania toward the Women Elementary School Principals," *Dissertation Abstracts International*, 27(5):1223A–1224A.
47. Shakeshaft, C., ed., p. 62.
48. Pigford, A. B. and S. Tonnsen. "Survey of Female School Administrators in the United States," unpublished raw data, 1990.
49. Shakeshaft, C., ed., pp. 83–84.
50. Shakeshaft, C., A. Gilligan and D. Pierce. 1984. "Preparing Women School Administrators," *Phi Delta Kappan*, 66(1):67–72.
51. Truesdale, V. 1988. "Employment Practices and Procedures Which Result in High Percentages of Women in Secondary School Principalships," Ph.D. dissertation, University of South Carolina.
52. Gross, N. and A. E. Trask. 1976. *The Sex Factor and the Management of Schools*. New York, NY: John Wiley and Sons.
53. McCarthy, W. M. and L. D. Webb. 1977. "Women School Administrators: A Status Report," *NASSP Bulletin*, 61(408):49–57.

54. Frasher, J. and R. S. Frasher. 1979. "Educational Administration: A Feminine Profession," *Educational Administration Quarterly*, 15(2): 1–13.
55. Shakeshaft, C. 1986. "A Gender at Risk," *Phi Delta Kappan*, 67(7): 499–503.
56. Doughty, R., p. 166.
57. Lightfoot, S. L. 1980. "Socialization and Education of Black Girls in Schools," in *Women and Educational Leadership*, S. K. Biklen and M. B. Brannigan, eds., Lexington, MA: Lexington Books, pp. 139–164.
58. Carr-Ruffino, N. 1985. *The Promotable Woman: Becoming a Successful Manager*. Belmont, CA: Wadsworth Publishing Company, p. 114.
59. Carr-Ruffino, N., p. 114.
60. Burbage, T. G. 1990. "A Study of the Use of Personal Traits in Teacher Selection as Perceived by South Carolina Secondary Public School Principals," Ph.D. dissertation, University of South Carolina.
61. Lynch, E. M. 1973. *The Executive Suite–Feminine Style*. New York, NY: Amacom, p. 92.
62. Loden, M. 1985. *Feminine Leadership or How to Succeed in Business without Being One of the Boys*. New York, NY: Time Books, p. 135.
63. Loden, M., p. 135.
64. Posner, M. J. 1982. *Executive Essentials*. New York, NY: Avon Books, p. 7.
65. Hummel, C. 1967. *Tyranny of the Urgent*. Chicago, IL: Intervarsity Press (quoted in Posner, p. 21).
66. Mackenzie, R. A. 1976. *Time Management Notebook*. Greenwich, NY: R. A. Mackenzie, p. 23 (quoted in Posner, p. 63).
67. Peters, T. J. and R. H. Waterman, Jr. 1982. *In Search of Excellence: Lessons from America's Best-Run Companies*. New York, NY: Harper and Row Publishers, p. 122.
68. Posner, M. J., pp. 27–29.
69. Dunlap, J. 1972. *Personal and Professional Success for Women*. Englewood Cliffs, NJ: Prentice-Hall, Inc., p. 56.
70. Kipling, R. 1920. *Rudyard Kipling's Verse, 1885–1918*. New York, NY: Doubleday, Page, and Company, pp. 645–646.
71. Loden, M., p. 203.
72. Loden, M., p. 191.
73. Posner, M. J., p. 47.
74. Peters, T. J. and R. H. Waterman, Jr., p. 119.
75. Loden, M., p. 182.

76. Loden, M., p. 135.
77. Hunsaker, J. and P. Hunsaker. 1986. *Strategies and Skills for Managerial Women*. Cincinnati, OH: South-Western Publishing Co., pp. 132–133.
78. Hunsaker, J. and P. Hunsaker, pp. 144–145.
79. Posner, M. J., p. 248.
80. Posner, M. J., p. 237.
81. Posner, M. J., pp. 239–240.
82. Doughty, R., p. 166.
83. Thourlby, W. 1978. *You Are What You Wear: The Key to Business Success*. Kansas City, KS: Sheed Andrews and McMeel, p. 1.
84. Loden, M., p. 65.

Index

Absence of accurate data, 2
Absence of role models, 12
Administrative certification, 30

Balancing your life, 41–49, 60–76
Black women administrators, 3, 13, 57

Carr-Ruffino, N., 28
Chancellor, W. E., 5
Communication skills, 49–54
Cost of success, 13
Crisis management, 46–47

Dealing with children, 71–72
Dealing with married men, 74
Dealing with single men, 75
Dealing with spouses, 69–71
Dealing with spouses of married men, 75
Delegation, 44–45
Doughty, R., 2, 3, 16, 58
Dunlap, J., 46

Evidence of discrimination, 2, 5, 6

Facilitating change, 54–55
Fear of rejection, 12

Hoyle, J., 5
Hummel, C., 42
Hunsaker, J., 51, 52
Hunsaker, P., 51, 52

Informal screening process, 15
Interpersonal relations, 39–41
Interviewing, 32, 34–37

Jenkins, W. J., 12

Keeping current, 61

Lack of confidence, 11–12
Leadership potential inventory, 23
Lightfoot, S. L., 17
Loden, M., 47
Lynch, E., 39

Mackenzie, R. A., 42
Making a speech, 52–54
Male principals, 3, 5, 13
Managing stress, 63–64
Marital status, 4, 12, 23–25
Meetings, 26, 42, 45–46, 58
Mentors, 28–29

Owens, E., 5

PETERS, T. J., 48
Planning for improvement, 46, 52, 53
POSNER, M. J., 42, 44, 48, 54, 55
Presenting a professional image, 61–63
Problems unique to black women, 16–18, 57–59
Professional image, 35, 61–63

RAMEY, E., 47
Resocialization, 9–10, 17
Resume, 31–32
Roles, 4, 11, 65–69

SHAKESHAFT, C., 1–3, 12, 16
SMITH, J., 5

Socialization, 8–10
SWIDERSKI, W., 5

Time management, 41–43
Time wasters, 42–43

Visibility, 13, 30

WATERMAN, R. H., 48
White women administrators, 3
Women in educational administration programs, 1, 2, 4, 6, 11, 12, 13, 18, 26, 27
Women's Institute, 11, 17, 22, 71

YOUNG, E. F., 5